RUNES

RUNES

AN INTRODUCTION

BY

RALPH W. V. ELLIOTT, M.A.

*Lecturer in English in the University College of
North Staffordshire*

MANCHESTER
UNIVERSITY PRESS
1959

© R. W. V. ELLIOTT 1959

PUBLISHED BY

MANCHESTER UNIVERSITY PRESS

316–324 Oxford Road, Manchester, 13

Printed in Great Britain at the University Press, Cambridge
(Brooke Crutchley, University Printer)

TO THE MEMORY OF

SIR DAVID RUSSELL

Kt., LL.D., F.R.S.E., F.S.A., F.L.S.,
F.S.A. (Scot.), J.P.

THIS BOOK IS GRATEFULLY
DEDICATED

CONTENTS

LIST OF ILLUSTRATIONS

PLATES

The plates are bound together at the end of the book

TEXT-FIGURES

MAPS

ACKNOWLEDGEMENTS

It is with pleasure that I record here the help which I have received from the following in obtaining photographs and permission to reproduce them in this volume.

The Trustees of the British Museum: Figs. 7, 10, 11, 13, 14, 15, 16, 18, 25, 34, 42, 43, 44, 45, 46, 47.

Dover Corporation Museum: Fig. 31.

The Royal Museum and Public Library, Canterbury: Figs. 26, 27.

The Rev. T. Romans, and the Curator and Council of the Society of Antiquaries of Newcastle upon Tyne: Figs. 30, 32.

The Rev. Canon H. R. H. Coney, Rector of Thornhill: Figs. 35, 36, 37.

The Rev. A. L. M. Maclean, Minister of Ruthwell and Mount Kedar Church: Figs. 38, 39, 40.

Mr A. P. Nelson, Mr D. Porter, and the Rev. C. K. Wrigley, Vicar of Hackness: Fig. 33.

The Rev. T. W. H. Rutherford, Rector of Bewcastle: Fig. 41.

Biologisch-Archaeologisch Instituut der Rijksuniversiteit te Groningen: Figs. 22, 23.

Friesch Museum, Leeuwarden: Figs. 9, 12, 20, 21, 24.

Lunds Universitets Historiska Museum: Fig. 19.

Altertumsmuseum und Gemäldegalerie, Mainz: Fig. 17.

Universitetets Oldsaksamling, Oslo: Fig. 8.

Musées des Antiquités Nationales, St.-Germain-en-Laye: Fig. 6.

Kungl. Vitterhets Historie och Antikvitetsakademien, Stockholm: Figs. 3, 4, 5, 28, 29.

Kunsthistorisches Museum, Vienna: Figs. 1, 2.

I also wish to thank the following for permission to quote from the books stated: Mrs W. G. Eddison and Sir George Rostrevor Hamilton (*Egil's Saga* translated by E. R. Eddison, 1930); Messrs Hollis & Carter Ltd. (C. W. Kennedy, *Early English Christian Poetry*, 1952); and Mr Edwin Morgan (*Beowulf —A Verse Translation into Modern English*, 1952).

The printing of this book is made possible by a gift to the University of Cambridge in memory of Dorothea Coke, Skjaeret, 1951,

PREFACE

RUNIC writing and runic lore are an interesting and valuable part of our Germanic heritage, and from the sixteenth century to the present day antiquarians and scholars of many countries have been fascinated by their mysteries. Not only the numerous extant runic inscriptions themselves, but the origin of runes and their several uses, the deeper meaning of the rune-names, the later history of runic writing in Scandinavia and Britain—all these have been the subject of devoted investigation and much fruitful, if often highly controversial, speculation.

In the Scandinavian countries, where by far the largest number of runic monuments survive, runic scholarship has inevitably attracted most students and made the greatest strides. The study of these monuments has progressed far since the days of Buraeus and Ole Worm, but the modern student still readily acknowledges his debt to these pioneers as well as to more recent Scandinavian 'rune-masters' like Wimmer, Bugge, von Friesen, and others.

In Britain the number of surviving Anglo-Saxon runic inscriptions is small compared to the wealth of Scandinavia; yet what we have is sufficient and varied enough to warrant study for its own sake. The interested layman will find in these relics of well over a millennium ago not only links with an even more distant past, but revelations of the culture and history of his forebears at a time not unlike the present, when paganism and Christianity were in conflict and the old and the new could appear side by side in a poem or on a tombstone. In addition, runic studies are an invaluable and sometimes indispensable handmaiden to the student of early English philology. The chronology of some early English sound-changes, for example, is considerably clarified by a comparison of early Frisian and early English runic inscriptions; and nothing surely is more beneficial and reassuring for the student of Old English than to turn from his abstract philological tables to the concrete evidence of actual inscriptions. Up to the present time, however, the English student has been hampered in his approach to runic studies by the lack of an introductory handbook on the subject comparable to those existing in German and the Scandinavian languages. Articles in English are few and not readily accessible, some are out of date. Nor do we possess as yet a complete and up-to-date edition of all extant British runic monuments to replace the unwieldy and in many respects antiquated tomes of George Stephens, invaluable though they are.

The present book, as its title is intended to convey, aims to be nothing more than an introduction to the study of runes in general and of English runic inscriptions in particular. It is addressed to the English reader who cannot readily make use of the standard works in other tongues, be it for reasons of accessibility or unfamiliarity of language. It is, moreover, designed primarily for novices in this field, and for this reason I have concentrated wherever possible upon what may be regarded as established facts rather than upon speculative theories. I may, indeed, be accused of occasional over-simplification for the sake of clarity and conciseness, but these are faults preferable, in an introduction of this kind, to complicated and controversial issues which might only confuse and discourage the beginner. Once he has mastered the fundamental aspects of runology presented in these pages, the interested student should be better qualified to pursue his studies into the more controversial fields of other and more advanced works. The same principles, coupled with the desire to present a fairly wide range, have guided my choice of English runic inscriptions selected for more detailed consideration in chapter VII. The experienced scholar will therefore find much in this work that lays no claim to originality; on the other hand I have not hesitated to put forward my own views or interpretations wherever I felt it right to do so. This applies particularly to some aspects of the question of the origin of runes and the interpretation of some of their names, and to the survival of runic lore in Scandinavia, Iceland, and England, during and after the conversion of these countries to Christianity, as well as to some suggested interpretations made in the last chapter.

My chief aim all along has been to stimulate an interest in the study of runes, to provide a good selection of photographs, and to do justice to our own runic heritage without neglecting the infinite variety offered by the Scandinavian inscriptions. If the following pages succeed in imparting to my readers not merely knowledge of new facts, but something of the unique magic of the fuþark, then I shall consider my endeavours liberally repaid.

The debts I owe to previous workers in this field are many and gladly acknowledged: to the work especially of Otto von Friesen, Wolfgang Krause, and Helmut Arntz; and to our own runic scholars and devoted antiquarians from John Mitchell Kemble to the present day. To Professor Bruce Dickins of Corpus Christi College, Cambridge, I owe a special debt of gratitude for active help and invaluable advice.

It is a pleasure also to acknowledge, with sincere gratitude, the generous financial assistance received from the Dorothea Coke Fund, from David F. O. Russell, Esq., and the Russell Trust, and from the University College of North Staffordshire. And finally I wish to thank my wife for her help in preparing the Indexes, and the Secretary of the Manchester University Press for his assistance and advice.

R. W. V. E.

KEELE, STAFFORDSHIRE
November 1958

ABBREVIATIONS

Gc. Germanic
M.E. Middle English
O.E. Old English
O.H.G. Old High German
O.N. Old Norse

An asterisk before a word denotes a reconstructed form not recorded. A macron or (in O.N. words) an acute accent over a vowel denotes length. Phonetic symbols enclosed in square brackets are those of the International Phonetic Association.

CHAPTER I

THE ORIGIN OF RUNIC WRITING

Modern Travellers report, that there are Runic inscriptions
now existing in the deserts of Tartary.

WARTON, *History of English Poetry*

THE word 'rune' suggests not merely a form of writing, the
angular characters of the old Germanic script long since dis-
carded, but a whole world of mystery and magic: strange
symbols scratched into ancient tools and weapons now lying
idle in some museum show-case; names of warriors, secret
spells, even snatches of songs, appearing on objects as diverse
as minute silver coins and towering stone crosses, scattered in
the unlikeliest places from Yugoslavia to Orkney, from Greenland to Greece. The word itself means 'mystery' and 'secret'
in early English and its related languages. When Bishop
Wulfila translated the Bible into fourth-century Gothic, he
rendered St Mark's 'the mystery of the kingdom of God
(iv. 11) as 'rūna þiudangardjōs guþs'. When the chieftains and
wise counsellors of Anglo-Saxon England gathered in conclave,
men called their secret deliberations 'runes', as does the poet of
the Old English *Wanderer* in a line weighty with wisdom and
secrecy:

Swa cwæð snottor on mode, gesæt him sundor æt rune.
Thus spoke the wise man in his heart as he sat apart in secret musing.

In *Beowulf*, the Danish nobleman Æschere is described as the
king's *runwita*, probably as distinguished a title as our privy
councillor. The German word *raunen* preserves this aura of
secrecy and mystery to the present day, while to *rown* or *round*
'in the ear', that is to whisper, was common English usage
until the seventeenth century, kept alive in more recent times
in the work of Scott, Carlyle, Kingsley, and other writers.

There is good reason why our word 'rune' should be so
heavily charged with overtones: runes were never a purely

utilitarian script; right from their adoption into Germanic usage they served for the casting of lots, divination, and other rites. Communication among people remained a secondary function of runic writing throughout its long history; much more common was the use of runes to invoke higher powers to affect and influence the lives and fortunes of men. It is not likely that both these functions derive from the same source, and in considering the origin of runes I propose to treat them separately: on the one hand the formal derivation of the characters themselves—runes as a script; on the other hand the magico-ritualistic significance of runes—the runic lore of the old Germanic world. The latter, I believe, had its origin in the pre-runic pictures and pictorial symbols carved into the rocks and stones of ancient Teutonic lands and closely linked with the religious beliefs and ritual practices of pagan Germanic antiquity. The symbolism of these primitive designs attached itself to alphabetic characters derived from quite another source, certain formal affinities facilitating the fusion. It was in this way that the runic 'alphabet' came to be primarily an instrument of magic and the storehouse of pagan Germanic rite and religion. The view that runes and magic were intimately linked has not gone unchallenged,[1] but there are weightier arguments in its favour than against it. Thus a good many runic inscriptions are obviously not 'secular' in the modern sense; the script, moreover, never lent itself easily to practical communication on any but the smallest scale, and it never developed a cursive variant; many literary references as well as the name 'rune' itself testify to the ritual uses of runes. These topics will be more fully discussed later on; for the moment our concern is with the formal derivation of the runic characters themselves.

The Germanic runic alphabet, or to give it its more usual name derived from the first six runes in their traditional sequence, the runic *fuþark* (*þ = th*), belongs to that branch of writing known as alphabetic scripts. In principle each letter

---

[1] For example by A. Bæksted, *Målruner og Troldruner: Runemagiske Studier* (Copenhagen, 1952).

represents a different sound; in practice, however, certain symbols are perforce employed for a variety of sounds, although the discrepancy between sound and symbol is not as far-reaching as, for example, in modern English.

The origin of the fuþark remains to this day the most baffling of all its mysteries. Many theories have been advanced ranging from the fantastic to the probable. The unhealthy nationalism of the German Third Reich unfortunately swelled the ranks of the former by trying hard to find a 'pure Aryan' origin not only for the runes but for all alphabetic scripts—'all writing, then, derives from the rune-hoard of the Stone Age...'.[1] Such nonsense we may safely disregard.

Only three main theories concerning the origin of the fuþark have ever merited serious consideration: those suggesting respectively Latin, Greek, and Northern Italic origin. It is probably correct to say that the last today commands most adherents, not because it is the most recent (it was first mooted a hundred years ago), but because the several related alphabets used in inscriptions found in the Alps, of the period from the fourth to the first century B.C., offer the most striking parallels to runic symbols, and because this view raises no chronological difficulties. These close parallels were already known to earlier runologists, like the great Danish scholar L. F. A. Wimmer, but were not used by them as a basis for explaining the origin of the fuþark. Wimmer's name is generally associated with the theory that runes derive from the Latin alphabet.[2] Briefly, this theory takes as its starting-point the several obvious Latin–runic parallels—notably the Latin capitals F, R, H, S, C, and the runic ᚠ, ᚱ, ᚺ, ᛊ, ᚲ —and then proceeds to derive the remaining runes from other Latin capitals. According to Wimmer this derivation of the fuþark was no gradual evolutionary process, but the creation of one man, much as Wulfila created the Gothic alphabet among the West Goths of the fourth century. The date is put by Wimmer around the beginning of the Christian

[1] E. Behrens, *Zur Herkunft der Runen und zu ihrer Verwandtschaft mit vorgeschichtlichen und geschichtlichen Schriften* (Leipzig/Strasbourg, 1941), p. 52 (my translation).
[2] *Runeskriftens Oprindelse og Udvikling i Norden* (1874).

1-2

era.[1] Superficially, Wimmer's theory remains attractive and it continues to enlist support,[2] but some of the suggested derivations make it very hard to uphold, and there is the added objection that the variable direction of runic writing would not easily spring from Latin writing which traditionally went strictly from left to right. This objection does not hold for the North Italic scripts.

Another theory that seeks the origin of runes in Latin script is that of S. Agrell[3] but, unlike Wimmer, Agrell turned to Latin cursive writing, that of the Pompeian inscriptions and its modifications found in the Roman frontier region of southwestern Germany whence, as in Wimmer's view, the fuþark travelled north towards Scandinavia. There are no chronological objections to Agrell's dating the origin of the fuþark *in this region* into the period A.D. 63–142,[4] but he places far too much reliance on rare and exceptional Roman letter-forms and is erratic in his search for 'original' runic forms, as he juggles to derive the twenty-four Germanic runes in this way. The fundamental objection, moreover, that a script as strikingly epigraphic and as little secular and utilitarian as the runic should have derived from cursive writing used largely for practical affairs is not satisfactorily answered by Agrell's arguments.

The Scandinavian scholar O. v. Friesen is the chief exponent of a view that places the origin of the fuþark among the Goths and derives it mainly from Greek letters, either capital or cursive, while some runes, not thus derivable, are assumed to be modelled on Latin letters.[5] According to v. Friesen, whose views (partly based on earlier suggestions made by the great Norwegian runologist Sophus Bugge) have gained large currency in the English-speaking world owing to their inclu-

[1] Thus in *Runeskriftens Oprindelse*; in *Die Runenschrift* (Berlin, 1887), p. 176, he suggests the third century A.D., which is too late for the earliest Scandinavian inscriptions generally dated about the same time.

[2] Thus, for example, H. Pedersen, *L'origine des runes* (1923), and F. Askeberg, cited below.

[3] *Die Herkunft der Runenschrift* (Lund, 1938).

[4] *Op. cit.* p. 29.

[5] *Om runskriftens härkomst* (Uppsala, 1904).

sion in the *Encyclopaedia Britannica* (1929), Gothic mercenaries familiar with both Greek and Latin adopted and adapted letters from both to write their own tongue, the result being the fuþark. This creation of the fuþark is placed in the Pontic (Black Sea) region in the third century A.D., whence, it is suggested, runes were carried north, back to the Baltic homeland of the Goths, leaving both archaeological and some runic evidence *en route*.

More recently, in 1944, F. Askeberg achieved something of a compromise between the views just outlined.[1] Believing with v. Friesen that the Goths were the first to write runes, although rather earlier (first century A.D.) than v. Friesen had assumed, he yet accepts Wimmer's suggestion of Latin origin as the most probable. An important point rightly stressed again by Askeberg is that the fuþark must be regarded as an individual creation rather than the result of an evolutionary development.

All the theories just mentioned have been criticised on various grounds which need only be briefly indicated here. Foremost are the formal or graphic objections against suggested derivations of individual runes from certain Greek or Latin letters; not infrequently such derivations are plainly *tours de force* intended to make the theory work rather than generally acceptable starting-points. Chronological and archaeological objections can be voiced against both Wimmer and v. Friesen. Modern runic scholarship is largely in agreement that certain northern runic inscriptions are as early as the third century, e.g. the Øvre Stabu spearhead (Fig. 8) or the Kårstad rock inscription. This rules out both Wimmer's later dating and v. Friesen's Pontic Goths: runes could not have been created in southern Europe at a time when they were already in use in Scandinavia. The Greek thesis is in any case the weaker, for not only does v. Friesen, like Agrell, depend on cursive letters and is forced to use some very exceptional forms, but he cannot even then dispense with certain Latin letters where the runic parallels are too striking to be ignored. Finally, the archaeological arguments upon which v. Friesen's theory largely rests have since

[1] *Norden och kontinenten i gammal tid* (Uppsala, 1944).

been shown to be far too weak to support any thesis of runic origin at all.[1]

There are two points which emerge from the preceding discussion: (1) the origin of the fuþark must fit in with the dating of our earliest known runic inscriptions in Scandinavia; and (2) certain Latin–runic parallels are too striking to be ignored, yet the Latin alphabet must be ruled out if particularly strained derivations are to be avoided and if the variable direction of runic writing is to be satisfactorily explained. But Latin writing had some close relations among the scripts in use in the Alps (the old provinces of Raetia, Noricum, Venetia, Pannonia), descendants of the old Etruscan alphabet, itself of still obscure origin,[2] and it is here that the origin of the fuþark has been most profitably sought. It is as well to be honest, however, and admit right away that no one definite prototype has yet been discovered among the alphabets used in the epigraphic inscriptions found variously around Lugano, Sondrio, Bolzano, and other relevant alpine places. A good many inscriptions have to do service before the fuþark is satisfactorily accounted for, but the possibility remains that such a prototype may yet be discovered: as so often, survival is accidental and exceptional rather than the rule. The thesis of North Italic origin was elaborated almost simultaneously by C. J. S. Marstrander[3] and M. Hammarström,[4] and has since been accepted by many runologists, in principle at least if not in every detail. The general basis of agreement may be summed up like this:

(1) There is an unmistakable resemblance between many runes and letters found in the alpine inscriptions (cf. Table I); this is probably not fortuitous.

(2) Some Germanic tribe must have been in touch with North Italic writing somewhere at some time.

[1] For an excellent, brief, critical summary of the whole question of runic origin, see F. Mossé, 'L'origine de l'écriture runique. État présent de la question', *Conférences de l'Institut de linguistique de l'Université de Paris*, vol. 10 (1950–1), pp. 50ff.

[2] M. Pallottino, *The Etruscans* (Penguin Books, 1955), pp. 257ff.

[3] 'Om runene og runenavnenes oprindelse', *Norsk tidsskrift f. sprogvidenskap*, vol. 1 (1928), pp. 85ff.

[4] 'Om runskriftens härkomst', *Stud. i nord. filol.* vol. 20 (1930), pp. 1ff.

(3) The creation of the fuþark must have preceded the eventual extinction of separate North Italic scripts by the Latin alphabet.

(4) From the Alps the knowledge of the fuþark must have been carried north to reach Scandinavia not later than the third century.

Difficulties and differences arise when we examine these propositions more closely. As for the derivation of individual runes it is probably safe to say that fewer formal and phonetic difficulties remain than in other theses. Reference to Table I will show that for three-quarters of the twenty-four common Germanic runes perfectly good parallels exist.[1] In the case of the voiced stops *b*, *d*, *g*, for which the Etruscan and alpine alphabets used the corresponding voiceless sounds, other sources had to be found, as in the case of the more specifically Germanic sounds *j*, *ė*, *ŋ*, and *þ*. Later in this chapter the point is made that whoever invented the fuþark was probably familiar with the pre-runic symbols found in the rock-carvings of Germanic prehistory mentioned earlier. Some of these symbols resemble North Italic letters and probably helped to facilitate the making of the fuþark; perhaps they even inspired it. In a few cases, I suggest, the 'rune-maker' went directly to these symbols to fill gaps in his model (cf. again Table I), notably ×, ᛇ, and ᛜ; ⋈ could also come from this source, or else from North Italic ⋈ *ś* with a changed sound-value. In the cases of F and B (both found in alpine inscriptions) we are probably dealing with incipient Latin influence. Finally, for ᛃ *j* Latin G *g* has been suggested, but I do not believe that our rune-maker knew the Latin alphabet. More likely we are dealing with another pre-runic symbol conveniently adopted.

The Germanic tribe responsible for deriving the fuþark unfortunately left no visiting-card behind: Marstrander thought of Marcomanni meeting with a Celtic prototype alphabet somewhere in the Rhine–Danube region; F. Altheim and E. Trautmann suggest that the Cimbri (or Cimbrians) met not only

[1] For a detailed study of the derivation of runes from known North Italic letters, see H. Arntz, *Handbuch der Runenkunde* (2nd ed.; Halle, 1944), pp. 35 ff.

Etruscan	North Italic	Runes	Pre-Runic Symbols	Latin
𐌅 v	F	ᚠ f		F
YV	Λ Λ V U	∩ Λ u	△	V
	ᛒ	ᚦ þ		D d
𐌀	ᚨ ⋀ ᚨ ⋀ △	ᚨ a		A
𐌓	D Ⴖ D	ᚱ Ⴖ r		R
>c ꓘk	< C K k	ᚲ k		< c
		X g	X	X x
	ᚹ ᚹ ᚨ ᚨ	ᚹ w		
𐌇	ᚺ ᚺ ᚺ	ᚺ ᚻ h		H
𐌍	ᛘ 𐌍 И N 𐌍	ᚾ ᚾ n	+	N
I	I	ᛁ i	I	I
		ᛃ ᛃ ᛃ j	ᛃ	G g
		ᛇ ᛇ ė	ᛇ	
𐌐	ᚴ 1 1 Ր Г Π L	ᛈ W ᛈ p		P
I ‡	ᛉ ᛉ ᛉ ‡ ✳	ᛉ ᛉ Ж z	ᛉ Ж	Z
𐌔 𐌔	ϟ ϟ ϟ ϟ	ϟ ϟ s		S
T +	↑ + T + ⊥ X	↑ t	↑	T
	B	ᛒ b		B
𐌄	ᚨ ᛖ 𐌄 ᛖ	ᛖ e		E
𐌌 𐌌	ᛗ ᛗ ᛗ ᛗ	ᛗ m		M
𐌋	Г 1 ᛚ L	ᛚ l		L
♀ q		◇ ◇ ♀ ŋ	□ ♀	
	ᛞ ś	ᛞ đ	ᛞ	
	ᛟ ∩ ᛟ ᛟ ◇	ᛟ o	⧗	O

TABLE I. Runes and North Italic letters.

North Italic writing but pre-runic symbols akin to those with which they were already familiar when in the second century B.C. they were warring in northern Italy.[1] H. Arntz assumes that, while the Cimbri helped to spread the fuþark northwards,

[1] In the Val Camonica rock carvings (north of Brescia) where, so it is assumed, tribes of Germanic origin had kept alive a picture-symbolism akin to that of the Swedish Bronze Age drawings in Bohuslän. Altheim and Trautmann, *Vom Ursprung der Runen* (Frankfurt (Main), 1939), pp. 47ff.

they did not originate it.[1] This was done from a North Italic source, he suggests, by one of the Germanic tribes variously reported in the north-western Alps by classical writers from Pytheas to Livy. This tribe, conveniently labelled 'Alpengermanen', came across North Italic writing in the fourth century B.C., evolved the fuþark from it, and in the second century B.C. passed the knowledge on to the Cimbri on their passage through Noricum.

Despite these divergences of opinion the outlines of the story are pretty clear. They become even clearer if we consider for a moment a valuable piece of evidence not yet mentioned. This is the inscription on one of twenty-six bronze helmets (helmet 'B' or No. 22) found in 1812 at Negau near the Austro-Yugoslav frontier, and first interpreted by Marstrander and P. Kretschmer. This helmet (Figs. 1, 2) bears in North Italic letters the Germanic words *hariχasti teiva*, generally interpreted as a votive inscription, 'to the god Herigast', which points to the conclusion that at some time some Germanic-speaking person or persons were sufficiently familiar with North Italic writing to use it for the words of their own language. As we have no evidence who these persons were and where or when, for that matter, this inscription was made, the helmet can do no more than act as a pointer towards the fuþark. The number of helmets found all together at Negau suggests a trader's depot perhaps, so that the inscription B[2] may have originated anywhere within the region of the North Italic alphabets. The phonology of the two words has also been criticised on the grounds that *teiva* (retaining the original Indo-European *ei*) is more archaic than *hari-* (from **harja*), but our knowledge of the chronology of pre-Christian Germanic sound-changes is not exact enough to doubt the genuineness of this inscription. There is no valid objection to our regarding the Negau inscription as evidence, first, that a Germanic-speaking tribe was in touch with North Italic writing most probably in the third to second century B.C.

---

[1] Arntz, *op. cit.* pp. 61 ff.
[2] Helmet 'A', or No. 1, has four inscriptions, all in North Italic writing, but no Germanic words.

and that, secondly, the fuþark was probably evolved between this date and the first century B.C.[1] For from the second century onwards Latin influence grew, causing a steadily increasing mingling of North Italic and Latin letters until in the course of the first century B.C. the alpine alphabets ceased to be employed. Latin influence can be seen in the creation of the fuþark, as has already been suggested, especially in the runes ᚠ *f* and ᛒ *b*, but such influence is not yet strong enough to warrant a date much later than about the middle of the second century B.C. This probably rules out the Cimbri, although not without regret, for we do at least know something about their movements in the later second century B.C. On the other hand it seems likely that they were far too busy campaigning to find time for the careful phonematic analysis evinced by the creation of the fuþark, and so rightly stressed by Askeberg. Had they found the time for such pursuits amid their wanderings it is very likely, as Altheim and Trautmann quite rightly admit,[2] that they would have chosen the Greek or Latin rather than a North Italic alphabet as model for a script of their own. On the other hand, the Cimbri may have been the agents that spread the knowledge of the fuþark northwards, when survivors of the battle of Vercellae (101 B.C.) returned to Germany.

Arntz's 'Alpengermanen' are admittedly attested by classical historians, but they are a shadowy crowd; we know little more about them than their willingness to serve as mercenaries to Celts and later to Romans. On the other hand, it is among such warlike wanderers that the Negau inscription probably originated.

Weighing all the available evidence we are, I think, forced to

---

[1] Views on the dating of the Negau inscription differ considerably, from the fifth century B.C. (A. Mentz, 'Schrift und Sprache der Alpengermanen', *Zeitschrift für deutsches Altertum und deutsche Literatur*, vol. 85 (1955), pp. 247ff.) to the time of Christ (P. Reinecke, 'Der Negauer Helmfund', *32. Bericht der röm.-germ. Kommission* (1950), pp. 117ff.). For a spirited vindication of the latter view and a suggested reading *Harigastiz Teiwawulfila(n)*, 'Harigast, son of Teiwawulf (Ziuwolf)', see H. Rosenfeld, 'Die Inschrift des Helms von Negau', *Z. deut. Alt. und deut. Lit.* vol. 86 (1956), pp. 241ff. Rosenfeld's thesis, although it affects the dating, does not materially alter the theory of North Italic origin.

[2] *Op. cit.* p. 47.

admit that it is not enough for a watertight theory on the origin of the fuþark. The outlines are there: the North Italic models; the period determined by the Negau helmet and the encroachment of Latin; the presence of Germanic tribes in the alpine regions during this period. But to try to fill in the details on the evidence before us has not so far met with full success, and there is real danger that the plausible thesis of North Italic origin will be discredited by a too rash superstructure of detail that suffers from lack of solid evidence and a too patent desire to make what facts are available fit into a preconceived scheme.

All we know then is that in some Germanic tribe some man had both the leisure (a factor often forgotten) and the remarkable phonetic sense to create the fuþark from a North Italic model known to him somewhere in the alpine regions in the period *c.* 250 to 150 B.C. Two questions, however, remain to which answers might be attempted: Why was the fuþark evolved at all and how was it spread, to the Goths, to the North Sea Germanic tribes, and to Scandinavia? Runic writing is not primarily utilitarian, so there must have been a different reason why it was created. Arntz,[1] to my mind quite rightly, suggests that divination and lot-casting were responsible for it, and we have the testimony of Caesar, Livy, Tacitus, and Plutarch to underline the importance of these rites among various Germanic peoples, as well as later evidence direct from Germanic sources.[2] Probably the maker of the fuþark belonged to a tribe familiar with pre-runic symbols already in use for sortilege. He met similar practices among some alpine people using their own letters: two-score wooden sticks with various North Italic letters and numerical signs have been discovered near Kitz-bühel, the famous resort in Tyrol.[3] It is difficult to imagine what else these could have been used for. An intelligent man our rune-master must have been, and he would soon see the advantage of using signs that could also spell words; so he set to work, and the result was a set of modified North Italic letters, influenced and in a few cases supplemented by pre-runic

[1] *Op. cit.* pp. 233 ff.   [2] Cf. below, pp. 65 f.
[3] Altheim and E. Trautmann-Nehring, *Kimbern und Runen* (Berlin, 1943).

Germanic symbols, the whole charged with cultic significance and linked from the start with religious beliefs and certain ritual practices.

The northward spread of the fuþark must also have been the work of some Germanic tribe; it would have meant nothing to Celts or Romans. Some Cimbrian survivors of the battle of Vercellae probably managed to recross the Alps and return into Germanic lands. There is evidence of Teutons surviving the battle of Aquae Sextiae (102 B.C.): their descendants reappear in the Neckar and Main regions of south-western Germany in the first and second centuries A.D. Altheim and Trautmann make much (too much!) of the so-called Toutoni stone, a rough sandstone pillar, about sixteen feet high, found near Miltenberg (Main, Germany), bearing the words INTER TOVTONOS followed by some cryptic initials too brief to be interpretable; beneath this inscription the authors claim to have found traces of a runic inscription.[1] Their case is unconvincing: one suspects that they wanted to find a runic inscription somewhere *en route* to the north to buttress their thesis and (considering the date of their paper) to claim for Germany the oldest known runic monument. But there is no need to look for runic inscriptions where there are none. Somehow the knowledge of the fuþark must have travelled north to reach Scandinavia by the third century, whether it was derived from the Latin or from an alpine source. The likelier route seems to be in the west, along the Rhine or partly through the present Württemberg (Neckar valley). Teutonic or Cimbrian remnants may have been the carriers, helped by Suebi and others; we can never know for certain, for even an isolated runic inscription could prove little or nothing. This way the fuþark would reach the North Sea coastal tribes and pass from them to Jutland, Scandinavia, and the Nogat Goths. On the other hand, it may have spread not only northwards but eastwards almost simultaneously, as W. Krause suggests.[2] Here lay the route of the Marcomanni to

[1] *Vom Ursprung der Runen*, pp. 74 ff.

[2] *Was man in Runen ritzte* (Halle, 1943), p. 8. Rosenfeld, *op. cit.* pp. 264 f., following a suggestion of Krause's, thinks that the inventor of the fuþark may have been a Vandal.

Bohemia, and beyond the routes of Vandals and Goths. Several early runic finds, all ascribed to the third century, have been assigned to these tribes; they hail from various places between the Pontic and the Baltic seas and could be due to migrants wandering back northwards. They include spearheads (Dahms-dorf, Kowel, Rozwadów), vessels (Niesdrowitz, Sedschütz) and the famous lost gold ring from Pietroassa.[1]

One of these inscriptions, that of the Rozwadów spearhead, has been tentatively interpreted as 'I belong to the Heruli', and it is worth concluding this chapter of conflicting theses and uncertain evidence with a reference to a people evidently famous for its runic knowledge. There are several extant inscriptions which suggest that at one time the Heruli must have excelled in the command of runic writing and the wisdom of runic lore that went with it. Such pre-eminence may have gradually turned the folk-name *ErilaR* into something of a title denoting the dignity or rank of a priest or sage skilled in rune-craft.[2] Thus the early sixth-century bone amulet of Lindholm (Malmöhuslän, Sweden; Fig. 19) bears on one side the words 'ek erilaR sa wilagaR hateka', 'I am a Herulian, I am called the cunning one'. By this time, however, the Herulian kingdom was destroyed, yet the name lived on in runic lore. Not much is known about these people: they appear to have come origi-nally from Denmark, ousted thence by the Danes. From the third to the fifth century, bands of Heruli are heard of in various parts of Europe, from Gaul to Moravia. It seems very likely that during these wanderings they became acquainted with the fuþark and took a share in its further spread, acquiring as they did so a reputation as 'rune-masters' and having accorded to them all the respect and privileges due to initiates into runic mysteries, all in fact that the title *ErilaR* connotes.[3]

---

[1] Details and illustrations of these will be found in H. Arntz and H. Zeiss, *Die einheimischen Runendenkmäler des Festlandes* (Leipzig, 1939), pp. 1-105, 421-30, and plates I-V, XXXVII.

[2] L. Jacobsen and E. Moltke, *Danmarks Runeindskrifter* (Copenhagen, 1941), col. 646. Cf. also cols. 817ff.

[3] G. Turville-Petre, *The Heroic Age of Scandinavia* (London, 1951), pp. 17f., 22f. For the view that the Heruli themselves invented the fuþark, cf., for example, P. Lauring, *The Land of the Tollund Man* (London, 1957), pp. 142f.

CHAPTER II

THE COMMON GERMANIC FUÞARK

He lette þer on grauen sælcuðe runstauen. LAȜAMON, *Brut*

OUR knowledge of the traditional sequence and the shapes of the individual symbols of the common Germanic fuþark, which consisted of twenty-four runes, is based on five runic inscriptions in which the fuþark is wholly or partly represented. The earliest of these and the only one to show the entire sequence of twenty-four runes, is the Gothic stone from Kylver (Gotland, Sweden) of the early fifth century (Fig. 3). Next in completeness come two Swedish bracteates[1] of the mid-sixth century, the one from Vadstena (Östergötland; Fig. 4) whose final rune, ᛗ, is not visible; the other from Grumpan (Skaraborgs län; Fig. 5), partly damaged so that several runes are partially or wholly illegible. Fourthly, there are extant the first twenty runes of the fuþark on a silver fibula, or brooch, of the later sixth century, found at Charnay (Burgundy; Fig. 6); and lastly, nineteen runes are preserved on part of a stone pillar found at Breza (near Sarajevo) and probably belonging to the first half of the sixth century.

On the two bracteates just mentioned the fuþark is divided with the help of dots into three sets of eight runes, which, following later Icelandic tradition, are generally known as *ættir*.[2] It is probable that like the entire fuþark the separate *ættir* were credited with some magic potency and that the numbers 3 and 8 played some part in the magic use of runes. Thus on the Lindholm amulet, for instance, the rune ᚠ occurs eight times in succession, ᛉ, ᛁ, ᛏ three times each in a line containing altogether exactly twenty-four runes (Fig. 19).

[1] A bracteate (Latin *bractea*) is a thin, round, gold medallion, stamped on one side, and generally worn round the neck as an ornament or amulet.

[2] From O.N. *ætt*, 'sex, gender, family, generation'; possibly derived from Gc. **ahti-*, 'set of eight, octave'. In the later Northern fuþarks of only sixteen runes (ch. III) the *ættir* consisted of only six, five, five runes respectively called, after the first rune in each, the *ættir* of *Freyr*, *Hagal*, and *Týr*.

Reference to Table II, p. 18, will show that the five fuþarks mentioned agree on the whole both in the sequence and in the shapes of the runes, although there are some noteworthy exceptions. Thus the Kylver fuþark clearly inverts the order of ᛢ *p* and ᛊ *ė*; but the evidence is less conclusive as to the original order of the last two runes: ᛗᛟ *do* or ᛟᛗ *od*. Later Anglo-Saxon runic alphabets show both alternatives. As to variations in shape, it should be noted that the traditional angularity and absence of curves and horizontal strokes in runic characters was due no doubt to their initial use on wood; as other materials came to be employed for runic inscriptions, considerable formal modification, such as the use of curves and horizontal strokes, was liable to take place. Moreover, as in the case of the North Italic inscriptions, there were no strict rules governing the direction of writing; therefore runes could face either way, to the right or to the left, and as on the Kylver stone both alternatives sometimes occur in the same inscription.

In detail the shapes and sound-values of the individual runes in common Germanic usage were as follows:

(1) ᚠ *f*. There is little variation in shape, but the Grumpan bracteate shows the rune curved to ᚡ.

(2) ᚢ *u*. Phonetic value as in *book*. The original shape may have been ᚪ, but ᚢ is generally found. The Kylver stone, which bears a short inscription apart from the fuþark, has this rune three times, with the shapes ᚦ, ᚴ, ᚪ.

(3) ᚦ *th*. Sound-value [þ] as in *thin*. Sometimes rounded to ᚦ.

(4) ᚨ *a*. Sound-value [ʌ] as in *but*. Sometimes shaped ᚼ.

(5) ᚱ *r*. Shows some formal variation, e.g. ᚱ, ᚱ, ᚴ, etc. The Charnay fuþark has the runes *u* and *r* practically indistinguishable.

(6) ᚲ *k*. This rune is invariably smaller than the others. A later development appears to be the turn to ᚠ as on the Breza fuþark.

(7) ᚷ *g*. The phonetic value was normally that of the velar voiced spirant [ɣ] as in O.E. *fugol*, 'bird' or Northern German *sagen*, rarely a stop sound as in *good*. There is little formal variation.

(8) Þ *w*. Sound-value as in modern English. Sometimes curved in shape to P.

(9) H *h*. The sound-value was either spirant, in Old English differentiated into palatal [ç] as in O.E. *flyht*, 'flight' or German *ich*, and velar [x] as in O.E. *dohtor*, 'daughter' or Scots *loch*, or else aspirate *h* as in modern English. Formal variants include N or ᚺ (quite possibly, in view of the North Italic variants, the original form of the rune), as well as N and H.

(10) ᚾ *n*.

(11) ᛁ *i*.

(12) ᛃ, ᛃ *j*. Sound-value as in *yes*. The shape of this rune was probably originally that just given, angular or curved, and 'half-sized' like *k*. As such it is found on a number of runic monuments which employ the common Germanic fuþark, like the Øvre Stabu (Kristians Amt, Norway) spearhead (Fig. 8), although by the fifth century the rune often reaches full height. The various shapes of this rune in the several fuþarks suggest gradual formal simplification by joining the two halves together, thus ᚻ ᚿ ⌐ N.

(13) ᛇ, ᛇ *ė*. The phonetic value of this rune, long disputed, is now generally assumed to be a high front vowel lying between *e* and *i*, representing an earlier *ei* (cf. the Negau inscription), which was probably still in existence at the time when the fuþark was evolved. In transliteration we distinguish this rune from regular *e* by placing a point above it.[1] The shape is quite regular.

(14) ᛈ *p*. The five fuþarks show considerable formal variation. It is quite possible that Charnay ᚹ represents the earliest form. The Vadstena bracteate substitutes ᛒ ᚦ which is characteristic of the later development of the fuþark in Scandinavia.

(15) ᛦ, ᛣ *ʒ*. Sound-value probably half-way between modern English *r* and modern English *ʒ*. Again in view of the North Italic parallels Charnay ✕ may represent the original form of this rune, of which the others are simplifications with the

---

[1] Professor Bruce Dickins suggests that the original value of this rune may have been *hw*, and transliterates ʒ ('A System of Transliteration for Old English Runic Inscriptions', *Leeds Studies in English* (1932), p. 16).

branches retained either above or below. Vadstena shows curving: Ψ.

(16) ϟ *s*. Voiceless sound as in *sea*. Generally found in this shape, facing either way, but more than three strokes, indeed as many as twelve, could be used for this rune, e.g. ϟ ϟ.

(17) ↑ *t*.

(18) ᛒ *b̶*. A bilabial spirant, still heard commonly, for instance, in the Bavarian dialect pronunciation of a medial *b*.[1] It is rather like the sound we make when blowing out a candle without rounding the lips.[2] More rarely a stop [b] as in *bird*. The shape allows some minor variation, such as Vadstena ᛒ, also ᛔ ᛔ.

(19) ᛗ *e*. Sound-value as in *end*. The shape is fairly regular, but the top stroke occasionally appears horizontal, ᛜ, or barely indented like the ᛗ of the Kylver stone.

(20) ᛉ *m*. Occasionally appears as ᛉ, approaching the shape of the *d*-rune, as on the Grumpan bracteate.

(21) ᛚ *l*. Occasionally found as ᛚ.

(22) ▢, ◇ [ŋ], the nasal sound of *ng* in *singer*. At first normally of half-size, like *k* and *j*, but a later variant, attaining to full height, is ᛝ. The ᛦ of the Grumpan fuþark is best explained as an incomplete specimen of this form.

(23) ᛞ *d̶*. Phonetic value [ð] as in *then*, rarely a stop [d] as in *dog*. The shape is quite regular.

(24) ᛜ *o*. Also appears rounded to ᛜ.

As has already been mentioned, the characteristic angular shape of the runes was initially due to their being inscribed on wood. The perishable nature of the material prevented large-scale survival of wood-inscriptions, but some have been preserved in the Danish peat-moors and the Frisian *terpen*[3] and there are references to such inscriptions in older Germanic literature. Apart from wood, metal and stone were the other chief materials for runic writing. Metal was used especially in connection with weapons, ornaments, tools and coins. Many such finds are extant and there are again references in the older

---

[1] Cf. E. Prokosch, *A Comparative Germanic Grammar* (Philadelphia, 1939), p. 76.
[2] Cf. I. C. Ward, *The Phonetics of English* (Cambridge, 4th ed.; 1944), p. 63.
[3] These are artificial mounds for dwellings erected by early settlers in Friesland as protection against floods.

	Kylver		Vadstena		Grumpan		Charnay		Breza	
1	ᚠ	*f*	ᚠ		ᚠ		ᚠ		ᚠ	
2	ᚢ	*u*	ᚢ		ᚢ		ᚢ		ᚢ	
3	ᚦ	*þ*	ᚦ		ᚦ		ᚦ		ᚦ	
4	ᚨ	*a*	ᚨ		ᚨ		ᚨ		ᚨ	
5	ᚱ	*r*	ᚱ		ᚱ		ᚱ		ᚱ	
6	ᚲ	*k*	ᚲ		ᚲ		ᚲ		ᚲ	
7	ᚷ	*g*	ᚷ		ᚷ		ᚷ		ᚷ	
8	ᚹ	*w*	ᚹ		ᚹ		ᚹ		ᚹ	
9	ᚺ	*h*	ᚺ		ᚺ		ᚻ		ᚻ	
10	ᚾ	*n*	ᚾ		ᚾ		ᚾ		ᚾ	
11	ᛁ	*i*	ᛁ		ᛁ		ᛁ		ᛁ	
12	ᛃ	*j*	ᛃ		ᛃ		ᛃ		ᚻ	
13	ᛈ	*p*	ᛇ	*ė*	ᛇ	*ė*	ᛇ	*ė*	ᛇ	*ė*
14	ᛇ	*ė*	ᛒ	*b/p*	ᛈ	*p*	ᛈ	*p*	ᛈ	*p*
15	ᛉ	*z*	ᛉ				ᛡ		ᛉ	
16	ᛊ	*s*	ᛊ				ᛊ		ᛊ	
17	ᛏ	*t*	ᛏ		ᛚ		ᛏ		ᛏ	
18	ᛒ	*b*	ᛒ		ᛒ		ᛒ			
19	ᛖ	*e*	ᛖ		ᛖ		ᛖ		ᛖ	
20	ᛗ	*m*	ᛗ		ᛗ		ᛗ		ᛗ	
21	ᛚ	*l*	ᛚ		ᛚ					
22	ᛜ	*ŋ*	ᛜ		ᛉ					
23	ᛞ	*đ*	ᛟ	*o*	ᛟ	*o̱*				
24	ᛟ	*o*			ᛞ	*đ*				

TABLE II. The five common Germanic fuþarks.

literature. In the Old English poem *Beowulf* the description of the sword captured by Beowulf and presented to Hrothgar contains the lines (1694ff.):

Swa wæs on ðæm scennum sciran goldes
þurh runstafas rihte gemearcod,
geseted ond gesæd, hwam þæt sweord geworht,
irena cyst, ærest wære,
wreoþenhilt ond wyrmfah.

Also on the hilt-plates of glittering gold
Was carefully charactered in runic letters,
Written and expressed for whom the good blade,
The spiral-hafted sword, the serpent-patterned
Had first been made.[1]

Rock-inscriptions are relatively few, but runes were frequently inscribed on stones, whether tombstones or memorial stones or more artistically shaped stone monuments like the Ruthwell Cross in Dumfriesshire (Figs. 38–40). Finally, mention must be made of the use of bone and horn; and in due course runic writing also appeared in manuscripts.[2]

The methods of inscribing varied with the material. The frequent use of the verb O.E. *wrītan*, O.N. *ríta*, O.H.G. *rīzzan* suggests that originally runes were 'carved' or 'scratched' into wood, metal, or stone; but more elaborate means of 'writing' followed, such as carving into wood, chiselling into stone, or stamping in the case of coins and bracteates. There is pattern-welding on some early runic spearheads: here the cuts are inlaid with thin metal wire, sometimes coloured red.[3] Colouring may also have been used on wood or stone.

As with most early alphabetic scripts runic writing normally recognises no division between words. Inscriptions could, as has been mentioned, read from right to left, or from left to right, or *boustrophedon*, that is in the manner in which a field is ploughed. Sometimes an inscription of two or more lines is to be read from the bottom upwards. Occasionally, however, various devices, such as one or several dots, were employed to distinguish either individual words or what might be termed

[1] Translated by E. Morgan, *Beowulf—A Verse Translation into Modern English* (1952).

[2] In the eddic *Sigrdrífumál*, st. 15 ff., are listed a variety of objects on which runes could be inscribed, including the paw of a bear, the beak of an eagle or owl, glass, gold, amulets, etc.

[3] Sometimes colouring may have been used simply to bring out the writing more clearly, or for ornamentation; but frequently the use of blood-red colouring had no doubt a magical significance. In *Grettis Saga*, ch. 81, the witch Þuríðr carves runes into the root of a tree, reddening them with her own blood and reciting spells over them to bring disaster to Grettir. The connection with magic is also stressed by the etymological relationship between O.E. *teáfor*, 'pigment', dial. 'tiver' (red ochre for marking sheep) and O.N. *taufr*, 'sorcery', O.H.G. *zoubar*, 'magic', already noticed by the brothers Grimm, *Deutsches Wörterbuch*, s.v. *Zauber*.

'sense units'. Reference has already been made to the use of dots for dividing the fuþark into *ættir* on the Vadstena and Grumpan bracteates.

A further point that requires mention is the use of ligatures, sometimes called 'bind-runes', that is time or space saving contractions of two (rarely three) runes into one symbol. The most common device is to use only one vertical stroke shared by two runes, as in ᚼ for ᚺᚠ or ᛉ for ᛗᚱ, but other types of ligature, such as ᛈ for ᛗᛁ *em* on the Torsbjerg (Schleswig) chape, are also found.

Double sounds, especially consonants, are not generally indicated as such in the older Germanic runic inscriptions, although there are some exceptions. This rule applies not only medially in words, but also when one word ends and the next word begins with the same sound.

CHAPTER III

THE RUNES IN SCANDINAVIA

Sigrúnar skalt kunna, ef vill sigr hafa,
ok rísta á hjalti hjǫrs
sumar á véttrimum, sumar á valbǫstum
ok nefna tysvar Tý.

Sigrdrífumál

THE runes of the common Germanic fuþark continued to be
employed for inscriptions into the eighth century, but already
before that time there appeared in the North changes both in the
shapes and sound-values of some runes, which in due course
resulted in a large-scale modification of the original fuþark.
Such modification, primarily due to linguistic changes, also
affected, as we shall see later, the runes employed in Anglo-
Saxon England; in Scandinavia, however, it took an unexpected
turn, for contrary to the development in England, the North
drastically reduced the number of runes employed, until there
emerged in the course of the eighth century two closely related
Northern runic alphabets of only sixteen letters each.

The seventh and eighth centuries were a period of rapid
linguistic change in the North,[1] and as the sound-pattern of Old
Norse was considerably altering as a result of such change new
sounds developed for which no separate script-symbols existed.
Of the two possible solutions—to create new symbols or to use
existing ones for several related sounds—the latter course came
to be adopted with the result that not only could one rune
designate as many as half a dozen or even more sounds, but
some of the traditional twenty-four runes fell into disuse altogether as their functions were either lost or transferred to
others. Already the Vadstena bracteate provides an example of
this: it no longer has a separate rune for the sound *p* but substitutes ᛒ (which it later repeats for *ð* to complete the sequence
of twenty-four), so that the one rune ᛒ has here the sound-values
ð, b, p.

---

[1] Cf. W. Krause, *Abriss der Altwestnordischen Grammatik* (Halle, 1948), para. 4.

The alphabet of sixteen runes which emerges in the North is known to us in two closely related forms, generally called the Danish and Swedish–Norwegian (or Swedish–Norse) fuþąrks respectively, both no doubt derived from a common source, and showing changes not only in sound-values, but also in the shapes of many runes suggesting a strong tendency towards formal simplification.

The Danish fuþąrk, probably the older of the two versions, is preserved complete on the Gǫrlev stone (Zealand, Denmark) of around A.D. 900. Its runes and their principal phonetic values are:

f	u	þ	ą	r	k	h	n	i	a	s	t	b	m	l	R

Further simplification, suggesting a slightly later stage of development, is evident in the runes of the Swedish–Norwegian fuþąrk, of which the best known example is the inscription on the stone of Rök (Östergötland, Sweden) which belongs to about the middle of the ninth century. The Rök runes are these:

f	u	þ	ą	r	k	h	n	i	a	s	t	b	m	l	R

A comparison of the above rune-shapes with those of the earlier common Germanic fuþark (Table III) shows that the simplifying tendency took the form of reducing most runes to one vertical stroke with a minimum of further differentiating strokes. The increasing use of runes for more practical purposes of daily life was no doubt largely responsible for such formal simplification; it led in due course to even greater economy in the so-called Hälsinge runes of the tenth to twelfth century, named after the district of Sweden where they mainly occur. These resemble a kind of shorthand, and were for a long time believed to represent no script at all. The guiding principle here appears to have been to omit as far as possible all *vertical* strokes, and to write what remained of the original runes between ruled lines where their position could indicate their value. The following fuþąrk, drawn from the Malsta stone inscription (Gävleborgs län, Sweden) of the latter half of the

Common Germanic	Danish	Swedish-Norwegian	Mixed	Hälsinge	Dotted Runes	Orkney
f						
u						
þ						
a	a	a	a	a		a
r						
k					k, q	
g						
w						
h						
n						
i						
j	a	a	a	a	a	a
ë						
p						
z	R	R	R	R		R
s						
t						
ð						
e						
m						
l						
ŋ						
o						
ð						
					c, z	
					y	
					ü	
					æ	
					ø	

TABLE III. The Northern fuþarks.

twelfth century, shows the extreme formal simplification attained by the Hälsinge runes:

f u þ ą r k h n i a s t b m l R, y

It has already been mentioned that most of the sixteen Northern runes carried multiple phonetic values, and these must now be briefly indicated.

(1) ᚠ denotes *f* and *ƀ*.

(2) ᚢ denotes principally *u, y, w*, as well as [o], [ø], [ɔ], *au*.

(3) ᚦ denotes both voiced and voiceless *th*.

(4) ᚨ, ᚨ denotes, from about the middle of the seventh century, the O.N. nasalised *á*, here printed *ą*, which eventually develops into [ɔ], generally printed *ǫ*, as the name of this rune illustrates: Gc. **ansuz*, 'god' becomes O.N. *ǫss*.[1]

(5) ᚱ denotes *r*.

(6) ᚲ denotes *k* and *g*, also the velar voiced spirant [ɤ] as in O.N. *fogl*, 'bird', and [ŋ].

(7) ᚼ, ᛐ denotes the aspirate *h*, and the voiceless spirant [x].

(8) ᚾ, ᚿ denotes *n*.

(9) ᛁ denotes *i, e, ė*, and [j].

(10) ᛏ, ᛣ denotes, from the sixth century onwards, the sound [ʌ], normally printed *a*. This is the original Germanic *j*-rune; the development of the rune-name Gc. **jēra-*, 'year, harvest' into O.N. *ár* shows how the loss of initial *j-* in Old Norse brought about the change in phonetic value.[2]

(11) ᛋ, ᛌ denotes voiceless *s*.

(12) ᛏ, ᛝ denotes *t* and *d*, also in nasal combinations *nt, nd*.

(13) ᛒ denotes the spirant *v*, the stop *b*, as well as *p* and the nasal combinations *mb, mp*.

(14) ᛘ, ᛐ denotes *m*.

(15) ᛚ, ᛐ denotes *l*.

(16) ᛦ, ᛁ, the original Gc. *z*-rune, regularly denotes in the Northern fuþąrks the strongly palatalised *r* (transcribed R) which developed in Old Norse from Gc. *z*.[3] In later Scandinavian usage—in some sound-combinations from the tenth century onwards, but not generally until the thirteenth century—this rune denotes [y], pronounced like German *ü*, as in its name *ýr*, 'bow made of yew', and here transcribed *y*.

From the early thirteenth century onwards a fairly uniform system of runic writing came to be adopted throughout the

[1] Cf. Krause, *op. cit*. para. 30.2.   [2] *Ibid*. para. 57.1.
[3] Cf. E. V. Gordon, *An Introduction to Old Norse* (2nd ed.; Oxford, 1957), p. 268.

Scandinavian countries. In the two preceding centuries the Danish fuþąrk had largely superseded the Swedish–Norwegian variant in Sweden, whereas in Norway a mixture of the two systems resulted in a fuþąrk approximately represented by the following line:

ᚠ	ᚢ	ᚦ	ᚬ	ᚱ	ᚴ	ᚼ	ᚺ	ᛁ	ᛆ	ᛌ	ᛐ	ᛒ	ᛘ	ᛚ	ᛦ
f	u	þ	ą	r	k	h	n	i	a	s	t	b	m	l	R, y

This mixed fuþąrk provided the basis for the common Scandinavian runic alphabet generally known as 'pointed' or 'dotted' runes, from the practice of adding points or dots to certain runes to indicate different phonetic value. The realisation that the sixteen-letter fuþąrk was phonetically inadequate must have prompted its deliberate extension by means of this device; thus ᛒ *p* was created by adding the points to ᛒ *b*, and similarly in other cases. One can see the influence of the Latin alphabet in the more obviously phonetic approach underlying the pointed runic script, as well as in the alphabetic sequence of the runes now adopted in place of the traditional Germanic order of the fuþark. Omitting certain regional variants, such as the system of dotted runes used in Gotland, as well as more sporadic formal variants, the standard Scandinavian pointed runic alphabet is as follows, based on the Saleby stone inscription (Skaraborgs län, Sweden) of the year 1228:

ᛆ	ᛒ	ᛌ	ᛑ	ᛂ	ᚠ	ᚡ	ᚵ		ᛁ	ᚴ	ᛚ	ᛘ	ᚿ	ᚮ	ᛒ
a	b	c	d	e	f, v	g	h, [x]		i, j	k	l	m	n	o	p

ᛩ	ᚱ	ᛦ	ᛏ		ᚦ	ᚢ		ᛣ		ᛎ	ᛐ	ᚯ
q	r	s	t		þ, ð	u, w		y		z	æ	ø

Scandinavian runic inscriptions are not only by far the most numerous; they are also the most widely scattered, for in the great Viking age (eighth to twelfth century) adventurous Norsemen carried their knowledge of runes from the Arctic Ocean to the Mediterranean and left runic evidence of their visits sometimes in the most unexpected places. One reason for the numerous extant Scandinavian inscriptions is the habit of carving runes into tombstones or memorial stones which have naturally survived in great numbers from the early Middle Ages and can be seen to this day in many parts of Scandinavia, especially in Sweden. Sweden has the lion's share of surviving runic monuments, between two and three thousand, while Norway and Denmark possess between three and four hundred each. Iceland, surprisingly, has few, considering the frequent references to runes in Icelandic literature, and none is earlier than the thirteenth century. To the same period belongs the dotted runic inscription on the stone of Kingigtorsoak, Baffin Bay, discovered in 1824, for long the only known undisputed runic inscription from Greenland. But since the end of the Second World War excavations on the site of a Benedictine nunnery beside the Unartoq Fjord and of farmsteads in the Vatnahverfi district have brought to light several rune-inscribed articles which include a carved wooden spoon and a whalebone fragment bearing in runes the name 'Gunnar'.[1] Even Baffin Bay does not seem to have been the westward limit of Viking expansion: some appear to have reached North America long before Columbus,[2] and 'runic' inscriptions have been produced to prove the matter. But despite much learned and often heated discussion the conclusion is inescapable that the Yarmouth stone in Nova Scotia is definitely not runic, and that the notorious Kensington stone (Minnesota) is a modern forgery.[3]

Turning from the extreme north-west to the south-east we find a most picturesque runic visiting-card on one of the marble lions that used to guard the entrance to the port of Piraeus in Greece. Here some Viking adventurers, possibly followers of Haraldr Harðráði, later king of Norway, perpetuated their

[1] See the account and illustrations by C. L. Vebaek in the *Illustrated London News*, 3 May 1952.

[2] There seems little doubt that the enigmatic *Winland* lay to the south-west of Greenland, i.e. probably Labrador or Newfoundland. Cf. L. Musset, *Les Peuples Scandinaves au Moyen Âge* (Paris, 1951), p. 226.

[3] Like the Piltdown skull, runes have been the toys of modern practical jokers. Among the most convincing runic forgeries was the inscription on a bone 'discovered' in Carinthia (Maria Saalerberg), for quite a time believed to date from the first century B.C.

names on this noble statue which was later, in 1687–8, carried off as loot to Venice. Another eleventh-century inscription hails from Berezanji on the Black Sea where a certain Grani made a grave-vault in memory of his comrade Kal, and duly recorded this fact on a stone: *krani kerþi half þisi iftir kal filaka sin*. Such runic finds clearly demonstrate both the distances travelled by the Viking adventurers and their readiness to perpetuate in runes either their visits or, more often, the names of fallen comrades. Examples nearer home can be found in the stones of Maeshowe, Orkney; here Rǫgnvaldr Kali, one of the heroes of the *Orkneyinga Saga*, stopped in the winter of 1151–2 with his fellow-crusaders and 'that man most skilled in rune-craft west over the sea cut these runes'. There are about three dozen runic inscriptions in Orkney, of which twenty-nine, all of the second half of the twelfth century, are in the prehistoric grave-mound of Maeshowe. Others have been found in Shetland, on the Scottish mainland and the Hebrides, in Ireland, and as many as twenty-nine in the Isle of Man.[1] And here and there in England are scattered a few more inscriptions to add to the total of Scandinavian runes.[2]

Gravestones and memorial stones greatly outnumber all other kinds of runic 'monuments' in the Scandinavian countries, but there is plenty besides: from crude pagan Germanic rock inscriptions of the third century to runes on elaborately carved Christian baptismal fonts[3] and other sacred objects. As examples might be quoted the twelfth-century Swedish Burseryd font (Småland),[4] with its inscription 'arinbiorn gørthe mik. uitkunder prester skref mik. ok hær skal um stund stanta', 'Arinbjörn made me, Vidkun the priest wrote me, and here I shall stand for a while'; or the beautifully carved Åker (or Åkirkeby) font from Bornholm (twelfth century), where the

---

[1] M. Olsen, 'Runic Inscriptions in Great Britain, Ireland and The Isle of Man', *Viking Antiquities in Great Britain and Ireland*, vol. 6 (Oslo, 1954), p. 153.

[2] Cf. below, pp. 38 ff.

[3] Cf. the Bridekirk font, Cumberland, with its early M.E. inscription in Scandinavian runes, and M. D. Forbes and B. Dickins, 'The inscriptions of the Ruthwell and Bewcastle Crosses and the Bridekirk font', *Burlington Magazine*, vol. 25, no. 133 (1914), pp. 24 ff.

[4] Von Friesen, *Runorna* (1933), pp. 233–4, fig. 66.

runes explain the figure illustrations much as on the English Franks casket.[1]

At this point two important facts come to light, namely that the Scandinavians were producing most of their surviving runic inscriptions at a time when elsewhere, in England, Friesland, Germany, runic writing was either dead or the antiquarian toy of leisured clerics; and secondly that a great many of these inscriptions are later than the conversion of the Scandinavian countries to Christianity. The reasons, I think, are these. In the first place, Christianity came late to Scandinavia, and secondly, when it did come it came to peoples so thoroughly accustomed to the use of runes for secular as well as ritualistic purposes that their conversion did not make any difference. After St Willibrord's abortive mission to Denmark in the eighth century came St Anskar (or Ansgar) in the ninth, 'but paganism was too deeply rooted among the Scandinavian peoples to be overthrown by one generation of preaching'.[2] Not until the end of the tenth century can Denmark be properly called a Christian country. In Norway and Sweden, with their many isolated and less accessible districts, the progress of Christianity was even slower: the conversion of Ólafr Tryggvason (in England in 994) was a milestone in the history of Norwegian Christianity but by no means the end of paganism; a more direct impulse came through the life and death of St Ólafr, Norway's first saint and martyr, whose veneration became the most solid asset of Norwegian Christianity.[3] In Sweden St Anskar had done some valiant pioneering, as he did in Denmark, but this left little, if any, trace and Sweden did not become properly Christian until the twelfth century. In Iceland the conversion to Christianity was a characteristically efficient and democratic matter: in the year 1000 Christianity was declared the island's official religion, yet certain traditional pagan rites were allowed to persist at least for a while.

By the time, then, that Christianity conquered the North

[1] Jacobsen and Moltke, *Danmarks Runeindskrifter*, no. 373, figs. 869–902. On the Franks casket, see below, ch. VII.

[2] G. Turville-Petre, *The Heroic Age of Scandinavia*, p. 85.

[3] Musset, *op. cit.* p. 129.

there had been centuries of runic usage throughout Scandinavia; a great deal of this was at least partly secular, especially the use of runes in Viking memorial inscriptions. The Church therefore could afford to be indifferent to runes, or else draw them into its service as it did on the Christian crosses and tomb inscriptions of the Anglo-Saxons. And yet there survived a good deal of pagan Germanic rune-lore as well: this is quite clear from the stories of rune-ritual and magic in the Icelandic sagas. Most of the great sagas date from the thirteenth century, yet they preserve intact a large amount of traditional lore that must have been very much alive at the time of the kings and heroes of whom the sagas tell. The saga of Egill Skalla-Grímsson may be taken as an example; its runic episodes are fraught with magic. In chapter 46 Egill detects a poisoned drink by scoring runes on a drinking-horn, reddening them with his blood and reciting a verse over them, whereupon 'the horn sprang asunder, and the drink spilt down into the straw'.[1] In chapter 57 Egill sets up a *niðstǫng*, a 'scorn-pole', against King Eirikr Bloodaxe and his queen, complete with the magic formula inscribed in runes. And then there is the often quoted episode at Thorfinnr's house where Egill sees a sick woman and discovers that someone obviously not skilled in rune-magic had placed a whalebone with the wrong runes into her bed:

Then quoth Egil:

> Runes shall a man not score,
> Save he can well to read them.
> That many a man betideth,
> On a mirk stave to stumble.
> Saw I on a scrapéd whalebone
> Ten dark staves scoréd:
> That hath to the leek-linden
> Over-long sickness broughten.

Egil scored runes and laid them under the bolster in the resting-place where she rested. It seemed to her as if she wakened out of sleep, and she said that she was then healed... (ch. 72).[2]

[1] *Egil's Saga*, translated by E. R. Eddison (Cambridge, 1930), p. 83.
[2] *Ibid*. pp. 174–5.

Other sagas have similar stories to tell, and in addition there are runic allusions and passages in the Eddic poems, like *Hávamál* and *Sigrdrífumál*, and references to other pagan rites and customs that went hand in hand with rune-lore. Many of these beliefs and rites survived the advent of Christianity; indeed it is quite fair to say, paradoxically, that the conversion of the North brought new life to paganism.[1] The new culture brought a new script, the Latin, which was less unwieldy than runes and which helped to transfer the oral literature of the North into manuscripts. But the cult of the past was not solely an antiquarian pursuit: there must have been many Icelanders after Helgi the Lean who believed in Christ and Thór and who believed in the efficacy of runes at the time the sagas were written much as Egill had done two or three hundred years earlier. And this persists much longer still: in seventeenth-century Iceland people were still burnt because runes were found in their possession, and it was necessary officially to prohibit the use of runes in 1639.[2] Elsewhere in Scandinavia where the conversion was slower and more erratic than in Iceland, the lore that went with runic writing must have persisted even longer. The conversion of the North, then, did not mean the end of runes; on the contrary, the great cult of the past, especially in Iceland, focused attention on runes and rune-magic, and our extant Icelandic inscriptions begin at this time, and, moreover, runic writing continued to flourish among Viking adventurers as well as in the homelands. A memorial inscription in runes must have had something of a sacred character: it was a link with kin and home and a past of which the Norsemen were proud; and it might (even long after the conversion) have had some protective powers ascribed to it— and all this Latin letters certainly could not do.

The runic inscriptions of the North are interesting not only for their own sakes and for the light they throw on Germanic beliefs and customs; they also provide valuable evidence

[1] Cf. Musset, *op. cit.* p. 132.
[2] Arntz, *Handbuch der Runenkunde*[2], p. 268.

regarding the original language of the Scandinavians and its changes and dialectal growth from the third century until Latin script takes over in the eleventh. Factual historical information these inscriptions rarely contain; usually they are too short and the persons named can hardly ever be identified. There are a few exceptions, however. Thus the two Jelling stones (Nørre-jylland, Denmark) tell us something of tenth-century Danish history in their terse runic lines:[1]

The first stone (about A.D. 935) has:

> : kurmR : kunukR :: karþi : kubl : þusi : aft : þurui : kunu
> : sina : tanmarkaR : but :

King Gormr set up this monument to his wife Thyre—Denmark's restorer—

whether 'Denmark's restorer' was Thyre or King Gormr is not clear; according to the evidence of history both qualify for the distinction.[2]

The other stone was set up alongside the first by Gormr's son, Haraldr Bluetooth, and its runes read:

> : haraltr : kunukR : baþ : kaurua
> kubl : þausi : aft : kurmfaþursin
> aukaft : þąurui : muþur : sina : sa
> haraltr ias : sąR . uan tanmaurk
> ala auk nuruiak
> . auk . tani karþi kristną

King Haraldr had this monument made in memory of Gormr, his father, and Thyre, his mother; the same Haraldr who won for himself the whole of Denmark, and Norway, and made the Danes Christians.

Two of the runic stones found at Hedeby (Schleswig, Germany), not far from the present Danish frontier, illustrate the value of runic evidence to clarify and corroborate the testimony of medieval historians, in this case Adam of Bremen, who wrote in the later eleventh century. The stones provide tangible evidence of Swedish supremacy in Schleswig under

---

[1] Jacobsen and Moltke, *op. cit.* nos. 41–2, cols. 65 ff., figs. 111–23.
[2] Cf. *ibid.* cols. 76–7, and Turville-Petre, *op. cit.* pp. 89 f.

King Sigtrygg, Gnupa's son, in whose memory they were erected and the runes carved.[1]

The linguistic value of the Scandinavian runic inscriptions has long been recognised: no earlier records exist in any other Germanic language and the earliest northern inscriptions cannot be far removed from Primitive Germanic, the ancestor of the several later Germanic tongues. As we study the runic word-forms we can almost hear sounds changing: on the fourth-century Einang (Kristians Amt, Norway) stone, 'Dagr painted the runes' appears as *đaga*R *þa*R *runo faihiđo*; about two generations later the same verb-form appears on a Swedish stone, that of Rö (Bohus län), as *fahiđo*, finally to emerge as O.N. *fáþa*. The whole process illustrates graphically what appears in the grammars prosaically as 'Prim. Gc. and Prim. O.N. *ai* became *á* before *h* which later disappeared'.[2] It is possible not only to study Primitive O.N. with the help of these runic inscriptions, but to watch the Scandinavian dialects developing and to make some estimates as to when all these changes took place. The famous Eggjum stone (Sogndal, Nordre Bergenhus Amt, Norway), for instance, suggests that by the early eighth century, when its inscription was made, this part of Norway had attained a phase of linguistic development well ahead of others and that many of the linguistic changes alluded to at the beginning of this chapter had already taken place.[3]

[1] Jacobsen and Moltke, *op. cit.* Haddebyst. 2 and 4: cols. 10–16, figs. 6–10, 14–21. Cf. Adam of Bremen, bk. 1, chs. 48 and 52.

[2] Cf. Krause, *Abriss der Altwestnordischen Grammatik*, para. 14.

[3] For details, see Krause, *op. cit.* where runic word-forms are frequently cited and conveniently printed in heavy type, and A. Jóhannesson, *Grammatik der urnordischen Runeninschriften* (Heidelberg, 1923).

CHAPTER IV

RUNIC WRITING IN ENGLAND

A king he was on carven throne
In many-pillared halls of stone
With golden roof and silver floor,
And runes of power upon the door.

J. R. R. TOLKIEN, *The Lord of the Rings*

THERE is no doubt that the art of runic writing was known to the Germanic tribes settled along the North Sea coastline among whom the origins of the English nation are to be sought. If the view suggested on p. 12 is correct, the knowledge of runic writing had reached these regions before its spread further north into Scandinavia.

The runes employed by the Anglo-Saxon settlers of Britain show certain modifications in form and sound conditioned by linguistic changes. Unlike the Scandinavian treatment of the common Germanic fuþark, however, with its reduction to sixteen runes, the Anglo-Saxon runic alphabets show an increase in the number of runes, reaching in ninth-century Northumbria a maximum of thirty-three runes. In the first stage of this development four new symbols were added, while the phonetic value of certain inherited runes changed. It is generally, and I think rightly, assumed that this process began on the Continent prior to the Anglo-Saxon settlement of Britain. As Arntz says: 'the more rapid linguistic development connected with the migration to new regions, with change of climate and mixture of peoples, must have led to the evolution of new sounds and necessitated new signs to represent them'.[1] It was probably on Frisian soil that the twenty-eight-letter alphabet evolved, for Old Frisian shared certain linguistic changes with Old English, and some of the new runes actually occur in Frisian inscriptions of the fifth to seventh century. Thus, for example, a small wooden 'sword' of the period 550–

[1] H. Arntz, in Arntz–Zeiss, *Die einheimischen Runendenkmäler des Festlandes* (Leipzig, 1939), p. 111 (my translation).

650, found in 1895 at Arum, south-east of Harlingen in West Friesland, bears the runic inscription ᛗᛇᚠᛒᛖᛞᛇᚱ *edæboda*, possibly a personal name or, perhaps more likely, a word meaning 'return-messenger' (Fig. 9). This shows a new rune for *o* in the fifth and for *a* in the seventh place, and a changed phonetic value, *æ*, for the old Germanic *a*-rune ᚠ.

We may assume then that the Anglo-Saxon settlers brought with them from the Continent a modified version of the older Germanic fuþark; and this is further borne out by the evidence of our oldest surviving English runic inscriptions. It is not, however, until the late eighth or ninth century that the first complete extant Old English runic alphabets of twenty-eight letters were recorded. There are two of these: the first *fuþorc* (so called to distinguish it from the older common Germanic fuþark because of the changed values of the fourth and sixth runes) is inscribed on a short sword, or *scramasax*, found in 1857 in the bed of the River Thames. This scramasax measures 2 ft. 4½ in. in length, has a single-sided blade and a long point; it is now in the British Museum (Fig. 7). Apart from the complete fuþorc it also bears the word ᛒᛖᚪᚷᚾᚩᚦ *bêagnoþ*, the name possibly of its maker or owner. The second fuþorc is recorded together with the names and phonetic values of each rune in a manuscript, generally associated with Alcuin, the so-called Salzburg Codex 140, now Codex 795 of the Österreichische Nationalbibliothek in Vienna. It is interesting to note that this codex also contains two Gothic alphabets, one of them complete with the only extant version of the Gothic letter-names.[1]

The two fuþorcs are as follows:

Thames scramasax

ᚠ	ᚢ	ᚦ	ᚩ	ᚱ	ᚳ	ᚷ	ᚹ	ᚻ	ᚾ	ᛁ	ᛄ	ᛇ	ᛈ	ᛉ	ᛋ	ᛏ	ᛒ
f	u	þ	o	r	c	g	w	h	n	i	j	ė	p	x	s	t	b
			5					10					15				

ᛖ	ᛝ		ᛞ	ᛚ	ᛗ	ᛟ	ᚪ	ᚫ	ᚣ	ᛠ
e	ŋ (=ng)		d	l	m	œ	a	æ	y	êa
	20						25			

---

[1] On the connection with Alcuin and the authenticity of the Gothic names, see R. Derolez, *Runica Manuscripta* (Brugge, 1954), pp. 52 ff.

Vienna codex

ᚠ	ᚢ	ᚦ	ᚩ	ᚱ	ᚻ	ᚷ	ᚹ	ᚾ	ᚻ	ᛁ	ᛡ	ᛋ	ᛓ	ᛉ	ᛏ	ᛒ
f	u	þ	o	r	c	g	w	h	n	i	j	ih	p	x	s	t	b

(numbered 5, 10, 15)

ᛖ	ᛗ	ᛚ	ᛝ	ᛞ	ᛟ	ᚪ	ᚫ	ᛠ	ᚣ
e	m	l	ŋ (=ng)	d	œ	a	æ	êa	y

(numbered 20, 25)

It will be noted that both versions preserve substantially the same order, except for runes 20 to 23 and 27, 28, and that this order clearly derives from the older Germanic fuþark.

The four additional runes are ᚩ *o*, ᚪ *a*, ᚣ *y*, and ᛠ *êa*.[1] The older *o*-rune still occurs as such in the oldest extant English runic inscription, a gold coin of the sixth century bearing the name ᛋᚳᚪᚾᛟᛗᛟᛞᚢ *scanomodu* (Fig. 11); by the end of that century, however, it acquired the sound-value *œ*, which by about A.D. 800 became *e*, a process reflected in the rune-name *ōþil* > *ǣþil* > *ēþel*, 'native land'.

The Germanic *a*-rune followed the Old English linguistic development and acquired the sound-value *æ* and the new rune-name *æsc*, 'ash'. Before nasal sounds, however, Germanic *a* became O.E. *o* as in the rune-name itself, **ansuz* > *ōs*. Both the position in the fuþorc and the name *ōs* were thus taken over by the new *o*-rune ᚩ. Finally, the new *a*-rune ᚪ was added and given the name *āc*, 'oak'; its shape differs slightly from that of some Frisian inscriptions, ᚪ, as on the Arum 'sword'.

The new rune for *y* is generally taken to be a combination of the two runes ᚢ *u* and ᛁ *i*, as it appears in the Vienna fuþorc. A number of variant forms, however, exist in Anglo-Saxon inscriptions. The name of this rune *ȳr*, 'bow', is not a common Old English noun and may have been adopted from Scandinavian.

The fourth additional rune is ᛠ *êa*. Its adoption cannot have taken place before the end of the seventh century, as there exist several Mercian coins, now in the British Museum, with the

---

[1] In the case of *êa* (also *to* and *ŝt* (cf. below) to indicate that only *one* rune is used) and *ŋ* (=*ng*) I follow Bruce Dickins's system of transliteration, as also for the Ruthwell Cross inscription in ch. VII. Cf. *Leeds Studies in English* (1932), pp. 15 ff.

3-2

inscription ᛈᛖᚪᛞᚪ *pada*, mentioned by Bede as Peada, son of Penda, who flourished A.D. 655–7.[1] Here the sound *ea* is still represented by the *a*-rune (Fig. 13).

Apart from these additional runes the following points should be noted. The sixth rune, ᚻ *c*, appears consistently in this form in the Anglo-Saxon inscriptions. It derives unmistakably from the Germanic rune ᚲ, the upper stroke being extended downwards until the rune attains the normal full height. Rune 12 represents the [j] sound and appears also as ᛡ, as in the name ᛡᛁᛋᛚᚻᛠᚱᛞ, *jislhêard*, on a Kentish (Dover) tombstone of the ninth or tenth century (Fig. 31). The thirteenth rune could face either way, ᛇ or ᛆ, and was used to denote either the high front vowel sound *ė* as in common Germanic usage and as in the Dover inscription just cited (where I have transcribed it *i*), or else the front spirant [ç] as in the word *almeᵹttig*, 'almighty', on the Ruthwell Cross, which will be discussed fully in chapter VII. This twofold function is suggested by the letters *ih* against the rune in the Vienna codex. Rune 15, the older Germanic *ʒ*-rune, had become superfluous in Old English and acquired through Latin influence the value *x* = [ks]. Rune 16, *s*, appears in various related shapes: ᚺ, ᚼ, ᚽ; the Scanomodu coin (above, p. 35) preserves an older form ᛋ. The *d*-rune appears as ᛗ in some earlier English inscriptions, for example the Scanomodu and Pada coins, but later commonly as ᛗ, as in the Vienna codex, or ᚺ, as on the Thames scramasax. Rune 24, *œ*, has normally the traditional shape ᛟ; the Thames ᚦ probably represents a simplified form.

In the second phase of Anglo-Saxon runic development a further five runes were added bringing the fuþorc to a final total of thirty-three runes. There is good reason for believing that this later development was confined to Northumbria and that it was not completed until the beginning of the ninth century; the Vienna manuscript, which probably goes back to an eighth-century prototype,[2] knows only the twenty-eight runes of the earlier English fuþorc. The Anglo-Saxon *Runic Poem* of the eighth or early ninth century adds to the twenty-eight-letter

[1] On Peada, see also below, p. 78. [2] Cf. Derolez, *op. cit.* p. 62.

fuþorc the rune ᛡ *io*. The splendid stone cross of Ruthwell (Dumfriesshire; Figs. 38–40), which bears in runes some portion of the Old English poem *The Dream of the Rood* and which may be assigned to the first half of the eighth century,[1] uses thirty-one runes. The final thirty-three-letter fuþorc was printed in 1705 by G. Hickes in his *Linguarum Veterum Septentrionalium Thesaurus*, vol. 1, p. 135, from the Cotton MS. Otho B x, which perished in the fire of 1731 when so many early English treasures were destroyed.

The five additional runes are as follows:

ᛡ *io*. In the *Runic Poem* its name is *iar*; *ior* would seem to be more correct, but neither form represents a known Old English word. This rune and its name are best explained as adoptions from Scandinavia. On the sixth-century Swedish Noleby stone, for example, the Germanic *j*-rune appears as ᛡ (Fig. 28). At the time of adoption into the Anglo-Saxon fuþorc the Old Norse name was **jár*, which became the Scandinavian name *ár*, 'year, harvest', but which in Old English became a meaningless *iar*, or *ior*, whence the sound-value *ia* or *io*.[2]

ᚻ *k* denotes the back-*k* as in *kwomu*, 'came' (Ruthwell), or in its rune-name *calc*, 'chalice'. Formally, this rune is clearly a modification of the *c*-rune ᚻ. The Ruthwell Cross uses in addition a special symbol for front-*k*, as in the word *kyniŋc*, 'king', namely ᛤ, transliterated by Bruce Dickins as k̄.

ᚸ *g*[u] is a modification of the regular *g*-rune, denoting the velar sound [ɣ] as in *galgu*, 'cross' (Ruthwell), transliterated by Bruce Dickins as ḡ.

ᛢ *q*, adopted through Latin influence and given the apparently meaningless name *cweorþ*. The value *q* is also recorded for the rune ᛣ, suggesting some uncertainty in the runic symbol to be assigned to *q* and also pointing to the relatively late date of this addition.

ᛥ *st* is the last of the additional runes. It occurs in a Frisian inscription of the later eighth century, the yew wand of Westeremden (Prov. Groningen, Fig. 22), twice in the shape ᛥ

---

[1] Cf. Dickins and Ross, *The Dream of the Rood* (4th ed. London, 1954), pp. 6 ff.
[2] Cf. also below, pp. 53 f.

and once as ⋈. As there is no ground for believing that this rune could have formed part of the original Anglo-Frisian extension of the common Germanic fuþark, its Frisian use suggests that the additional Northumbrian runes found their way back to Friesland towards the end of the eighth century.

We thus obtain the following thirty-three-letter fuþorc in use in Northumbria about the year 800:

f	u	þ	o	r	c	g¹	w	h	n	i	j	ė/[ç]	p	x	s	t

b	e	m	l	ŋ	œ	d	a	æ	y	êa	îo	k	gⁿ	q	ŝt

For ease of comparison several Anglo-Saxon fuþorcs are listed, together with the original twenty-four Germanic runes, in Table IV.

The advent of the Viking Age and the beginnings of the Scandinavian raids on Britain, and the eventual settlement of Norsemen on British soil, brought to this country the runic characters then current in Scandinavia. We have already seen, in the previous chapter, that the majority of Scandinavian inscriptions in the British Isles are in Orkney[1] and in the Isle of Man.[2] The fuþąrks used are modifications of the two main Scandinavian types: that found in most of the Manx inscriptions derives from the Swedish–Norwegian type and is sometimes referred to as the 'Man-Jær' type,[3] whereas the Maeshowe inscriptions use a fuþąrk derived mainly from the Danish type, also called the 'Common' or 'Older Norse' fuþąrk (cf. Table III, p. 23).

The best-known examples of Scandinavian runes in England are the eleventh-century sculptured stone found in St Paul's churchyard and now in the Guildhall Museum, which records that 'Finna and Toki had this stone set up'; and the *þorfastr*

---

[1] See especially the Royal Commission on the Ancient Monuments of Scotland, 12th Report, 3 vols. (Edinburgh, 1946). On Maeshowe, see vol. 2, pp. 306 ff.

[2] P. M. C. Kermode, *Manx Crosses* (London, 1907), and Olsen, *op. cit.* pp. 182 ff.

[3] Olsen, *op. cit.* pp. 155 ff.

	Common Germanic		Thames		Vienna		Cod. Otho B X (10th century)		Ruthwell	
1	ᚠ	f	ᚠ		ᚠ		ᚠ		ᚠ	
2	ᚢ	u	ᚢ		ᚢ		ᚢ		ᚢ	
3	ᚦ	þ	ᚦ		ᚦ		ᚦ		ᚦ	
4	ᚨ	a	ᚩ	o	ᚩ	o	ᚩ	o	ᚩ	o
5	ᚱ	r	ᚱ		ᚱ		ᚱ		ᚱ	
6	ᚲ	k	ᚳ	c	ᚳ	c	ᚳ	c	ᚳ	c
7	ᚷ	g	ᚷ		ᚷ		ᚷ		ᚷ	
8	ᚹ	w	ᚹ		ᚹ		ᚹ		ᚹ	
9	ᚺ	h	ᚻ		ᚻ		ᚻ ᚼ ᚺ		ᚻ	
10	ᚾ	n	ᚾ		ᚾ		ᚾ ᚾ		ᚾ	
11	ᛁ	i	ᛁ		ᛁ		ᛁ		ᛁ	
12	ᛃ	j	+		ᛄ		ᛄ			
13	ᛇ	ė	ᛇ	ė	ᛇ	'ih'	S ᛇ	'eo'	ᛇ	[ç]
14	ᛈ	p	ᛈ		ᛈ		ᛈ			
15	ᛉ	z	ᛉ	x	ᛉ	x	ᛉ	x		
16	ᛊ	s	ᛋ		ᛋ		ᛋ		ᛋ	
17	ᛏ	t	ᛏ		ᛏ		ᛏ		ᛏ	
18	ᛒ	b	ᛒ	b	ᛒ	b	ᛒ	b	ᛒ	b
19	ᛖ	e	ᛖ		ᛖ		ᛖ		ᛖ	
20	ᛗ	m	ᛝ	ŋ	ᛗ	m	ᛗ	m	ᛗ	m
21	ᛚ	l	ᛞ	d	ᛚ	l	ᛚ	l	ᛚ	l
22	ᛜ	ŋ	ᛚ	l	ᛝ	ŋ	ᛝ ᛝ	ŋ	ᛝ	ŋ
23	ᛟ	o	ᛗ	m	ᛞ	d	ᛟ	œ	ᛟ	œ
24	ᛞ	đ	ᛟ	œ	ᛟ	œ	ᛞ	d	ᛞ	d
25			ᚪ	a	ᚪ	a	ᚪ	a	ᚪ	a
26			ᚫ	æ	ᚫ	æ	ᚫ	æ	ᚫ	æ
27			ᚣ	y	ᛠ	êa	ᚣ	y	ᚣ	y
28			ᛠ	êa	ᚣ	y	ᛡ	îo	ᛠ	êa
29							ᛠ	êa	ᛣ	k^{I}
30							ᛢ	q	ᛤ	k^{II}
31							ᛣ	k	ᚸ	g^{II}
32							ᛥ	ŝt		
33							ᚸ	g^{II}		

TABLE IV. Old English fuþorcs and the Ruthwell runes.

comb from Lincoln (Fig. 47), now in the British Museum, so called because the maker of the comb took good care to perpetuate his name on it.[1] The latter is a Danish inscription; others, of Norwegian origin, have come to light in several places in Yorkshire, Cumberland, and Lancashire, such as the inscribed stone in Carlisle Cathedral, the runes on the tym-

[1] Jacobsen and Moltke, *op. cit.* no. 418, col. 488, fig. 1034.

panum of Pennington (Furness) church, and those from Thornaby-on-Tees, all of the twelfth century. The curiously mixed Anglo-Norse inscription of the Bridekirk (Cumberland) font has already been mentioned.

The Manx runes are mainly inscribed on crosses and cross fragments, and are nearly all formulaic memorial inscriptions of the type 'So-and-So set up this cross after (in memory of) So-and-So', various relatives qualifying for such distinction: father, mother, foster-mother, wife, son, daughter. One inscription, Braddan II, is exceptional in commemorating a death due to treachery.[1] A typical example is Andreas II: 'sạnt : ulf : hin : suarti : raisti : krus þạna : aftir : arin : biau(r)k · kuinu (:)sina(:)', 'Sandulf the Black erected this cross after Arinbiǫrg his wife'.[2] Two inscriptions in Anglo-Saxon runes have also been found in the Isle of Man, and there are several others in Ogham (or Ogom) characters.[3] The Manx runic inscriptions belong in the main to the tenth to twelfth century.

St Augustine and his monks arrived in Kent in A.D. 597 to begin the task of converting the heathen English. Superficially, their success seemed quick and assured, but beneath the converted surface there probably lurked for a long time a much larger residue of paganism than Bede's account or those of later historians would have us believe. In the middle of the eighth century (A.D. 747) the Council of Clofeshoh found it necessary to condemn those who practised heathen rites of divination, incantations, and the like; and eighth-century poems, like the 'elegiac' *Wanderer* or *Seafarer* pay as yet only lip-service to Christianity: the full assurance, the firm faith of genuine con-

---

[1] Olsen, *op. cit.* p. 191.   [2] *Ibid.* p. 184.

[3] Ogham is a form of alphabetic writing used for inscriptions belonging in the main to the fifth to eighth century and found only in the British Isles. Its letters are formed by a systematic use of vertical, horizontal, and diagonal strokes. There are several varieties of Ogham writing, of which the best known is *Ogam Craobh*, 'Tree Ogham'. A connection with runic writing has been suggested, but is highly speculative. Cf., for example, H. Arntz, 'Das Ogom', *Beiträge z. Gesch. deut. Sprache und Literatur*, vol. 59 (1935), pp. 321 ff.; R. Thurneysen, 'Zum Ogom', *ibid.* vol. 61 (1937), pp. 188 ff.; J. Vendryes, 'L'écriture ogamique et ses origines', *Études Celtiques*, vol. 4 (1941), pp. 83 ff.; R. A. S. Macalister, *Corpus inscriptionum insularum celticarum.* (Irish Manuscripts Commission. 3 vols. Dublin, 1945–49).

version are not yet theirs. Together with other relics of the pagan past, runes survive well into Christian England, just as they did in Scandinavia. There are two reasons for this: on the one hand the politic tolerance of the early Church, on the other hand the instinctive traditionalism of the people, who have clung to many familiar beliefs and superstitious practices not only throughout the Middle Ages, but well into our own times. Pope Gregory's advice to the early missionaries was to mingle their evangelistic zeal with moderation, to adapt and adopt things pagan whenever possible rather than antagonise the people into active opposition by too violent a policy.[1] There was good cause for such advice, for 'heathenism was both widespread and deeply-rooted among the English when Augustine reached Canterbury in 597'.[2] The study of English place-names has revealed numerous places sacred to Germanic deities or ritual and it is not unlikely that some Anglo-Saxon churches were built on sites of pagan fanes or sacred groves as Gregory had advocated.[3] The cult of the yew tree, inherited from the Celts, probably played its part in this development: from Anglo-Saxon times onwards yews, long associated with pagan ritual and superstition, came to be commonly connected with churches and churchyards, and some ancient yew-rites were taken over into Christian observance.[4] Runic lore and magic were part of the inheritance of the Anglo-Saxons and they lived on among the people long after the coming of the missionaries. Little such 'folklore' found its way into writing, unfortunately, and recorded evidence is thus inevitably scanty, but some indications exist of the place of runes in popular tradition. In certain Old English charms, where the reciting of the spell went hand in hand with ritual gestures, runes or allusions to runes occur.[5] To the ninth century belong the runic

---

[1] Cf. Bede, *Historia Ecclesiastica*, I, 27, 30.

[2] P. Hunter Blair, *An Introduction to Anglo-Saxon England* (Cambridge, 1956), p. 123. Cf. also B. Branston, *The Lost Gods of England* (London, 1957), *passim*.

[3] Bede, *op. cit.* I, 30. E. A. Philippson, *Germanisches Heidentum bei den Angel-sachsen* (Leipzig, 1929), p. 184.

[4] R. W. V. Elliott, 'Runes, Yews, and Magic', *Speculum*, vol. 32 (1957), pp. 250ff.

[5] For example, G. Storms, *Anglo-Saxon Magic* (The Hague, 1948), nos. 9, 33.

passages in Cynewulf's poems and the Old English *Runic Poem* with unmistakable echoes of Germanic rune-lore in their rune-names; another Old English poem, *Solomon and Saturn*, shows a learned adaptation to Christian use of the age-old belief in the magic efficacy of runes. The Germanic customs of divination and sortilege, often no doubt involving runes, survive into modern times in the secular custom of casting lots for hides found in some English parishes. Some of the marks used there are runes, as are some of the traditional English merchants' and masons' marks.[1] Such survivals, scanty though admittedly they are, reveal something of the popular persistence of runic lore. Meanwhile runic writing as such was drawn into the service of the Church: as in the Scandinavian countries, so in England, runes came to be used on Christian gravestones and other sacred monuments, of which the Ruthwell cross in Dumfriesshire is our finest example (Figs. 38–40). Gradually inscriptions of a mixed character appear, drawing both on the Latin alphabet and on the fuþorc. Probably the earliest of these is the inscription on St Cuthbert's coffin at Durham of about A.D. 700, followed in due course by series of coins. A typical example is the inscription ᛒᛖᚩᛏᛏᚾ REX *Beonna Rex* of an East Anglian coin, referring to Beonna or Beorna who flourished, according to Florence of Worcester, in A.D. 758. Here the majority of the letters are drawn from the Latin alphabet (Fig. 15).

One of the results of the conversion of England was the establishment of monastic scriptoria all over the country. It is here that runes became a bookish pursuit, first merely an orthographic convenience in the writing of the vernacular, but later an antiquarian pastime for its own sake; alphabet lore and cryptic writing had, it seems, a particular fascination for medieval minds: as late as the second half of the fourteenth century weird alphabets based on the fuþorc appear in *Sir John Mandeville's Travels*,[2] with quite clearly a long monkish tradition

---

[1] Elliott, *op. cit.* p. 260.

[2] M. Letts, *Sir John Mandeville. The Man and his Book* (London, 1949), ch. XVII, pl. xv. Cf. Derolez, *op. cit.* pp. 275 ff.

behind them. To the scribal knowledge of runes we owe the adoption of the runes Þ *th* and Ƿ *w* into the regular minuscule script of Anglo-Saxon England. The latter was in due course replaced by the continental *w*, but the former, the 'thorn' rune, persisted throughout the Middle Ages approaching increasingly the shape of our letter *y* and becoming finally identified with it in forms like 'yᵉ' for 'the' and 'yᵗ' for 'that', still visible today all over the country on signs of the 'Ye Olde Tea Shoppe' type. The 'thorn' rune still forms part of modern Icelandic writing today. Apart from these two runes Anglo-Saxon scribes made use of others for purposes of shorthand, as happened also in Scandinavia, writing the rune where the meaning denoted by the name was required, thus ᛗ *mon*, 'man', ᛗ *dæg*, 'day', ᛟ *œþel*, *eþel*, 'native land'.[1] Cynewulf uses the same device to conceal or rather reveal his name in three of his four signed poems, and the same principle is also employed for acrostic purposes in some of the Riddles of the Exeter Book of Old English poems.

The antiquarian interest in runes speaks out of the several extant manuscript fuþorcs discovered in various English and continental codices. Some of these are linked to a short treatise on cryptography, the so-called *Isruna Tract*; in other cases the fuþorcs have been transposed into runic alphabets, some of them forming part of a short treatise on the history of the alphabet.[2] All this 'points evidently to the scholar's study; it is utterly remote from runic tradition'.[3] At some stage, clearly, a live popular tradition of the epigraphic use of runes coupled with magico-ritualistic beliefs and practices became, in part at least, 'bookish'. Cynewulf's acrostic use of runes to spell his name, the runic Riddles, and the cryptic runic message in the Anglo-Saxon poem, *The Husband's Message*, lie somewhere along this road. They still echo, just as the Icelandic poems and sagas do, something of the genuine runic usages of earlier generations—their mystery, secrecy, concealment; their employment

---

[1] Thus, for example, in the manuscript of *Beowulf*, ll. 520, 913, 1702, of the edited text, or *Waldere*, 31, etc.

[2] Derolez, *op. cit.* chs. I–IV.   [3] *Ibid.* p. 430.

for brief messages on a rune-staff; the symbolical or pagan-religious associations of some of the rune-names—all these belong to the time when runes were still a living script. That so few English manuscript runes exist is due, as Derolez rightly points out, to the fact that as runes were fairly widely known there was little need to write them down: 'Runes were part of the intellectual pattern.'[1] In continental manuscripts a great deal more material survives; presumably runes were part of the equipment of traders and adventurers who plied between England and the Continent, and later of Anglo-Saxon missionaries also. In the latter case no question of rune-magic arises; instead we have here a link between an originally alive and meaningful runic tradition on the one hand and the dead, bookish runes of the continental manuscript fuþorcs and alphabets on the other.

When the epigraphic use of Anglo-Saxon runes ceased in England is impossible to determine for certain. The Dover stone is probably late ninth or early tenth century.[2] The Overchurch inscription in the Chester Museum may also be fairly late; it depends on who the Æthelmund is for whom it requests prayer. The tenth century, with its renewed evangelical fervour and monastic expansion, probably saw the end of runic epigraphy as far as the Anglo-Saxons were concerned, while the Scandinavians carried on their own runic traditions on British soil for several centuries longer.

[1] Derolez, *op. cit.* p. 426. [2] Cf. below, pp. 82f.

CHAPTER V

THE NAMES OF THE RUNES

Beneath the shade the Northmen came,
Fixed on each vale a Runic name.
SCOTT, Rokeby

OUR word 'alphabet' derives from the first two letters of the Greek alphabet, *alpha* and *beta*, in their turn adopted from the Semitic *aleph* and *beth*. In Semitic the names of the letters were meaningful words, in Greek they functioned solely as letter-names. Like the Semitic letters the Germanic runes possessed names which formed part of the vocabulary of ordinary speech, and it was no uncommon practice to make a single rune stand for its name-word, whether for purposes of magic as on the Lindholm amulet, or as an occasional form of shorthand as in some Anglo-Saxon and Norse manuscripts. In nearly every case the rune-names begin with the same sound which the rune denoted in normal alphabetic usage.

The names of the Germanic runes are not preserved in any early runic inscription; the later manuscript versions, however, both English and continental, show such a measure of agreement in the forms and meanings of the names that an early common origin cannot be disputed.[1] In addition to these manuscript lists of runes and their names there exist four runic poems, one of them Old English of the ninth century, in which the names of the separate runes are made the subjects of short poetic stanzas.[2] Finally, there is the Vienna codex previously mentioned in which the letters of the Gothic alphabet, evolved by Bishop Wulfila in the fourth century, are accompanied by names which, however dubious some of the forms appear, betray an unmistakable affinity with the rune-names preserved in other sources. It is most likely that when the Gothic alpha-

---

[1] For the fullest and most up-to-date treatment of these, see R. Derolez, *Runica Manuscripta*.

[2] The best edition of the runic poems is Bruce Dickins, *Runic and Heroic Poems of the Old Teutonic Peoples* (Cambridge, 1915).

bet was first developed the traditional Germanic rune-names were conveniently adopted as names for the letters.

For easy comparison the names of the Gothic letters and the names of the runes derived from various sources are listed in Table V (pp. 48–9). The reader will see at once that the parallels revealed are too striking to be purely fortuitous. As the Scandinavian fuþąrks reduced their number of runes only sixteen rune-names exist in their Northern form; nonetheless, there can be no doubt that originally all twenty-four runes of the common Germanic fuþark possessed names.[1] These are probably largely preserved in the Anglo-Saxon rune-names, although the names of the additional Anglo-Saxon runes must be regarded as later creations.

It will be noticed that in some cases the meanings of the rune-names differ in our various sources, even where the forms are etymologically the same, while in others cases different etymologies apply. Thus ∩ *u* probably had the original Germanic name **ūruz*, 'aurochs', still retained in the Old English runic poem, but replaced by more familiar homonyms meaning 'slag' and 'drizzle' in the Old Norwegian and Old Icelandic runic poems respectively. A substitution prompted perhaps by Christian motives took place in the case of Þ *th*, Gc. **þurisaz*, 'giant, demon', retained in the Scandinavian poems, but replaced by the more innocuous *þorn*, 'thorn', in Old English. As the meanings of some of the older rune-names were forgotten or perhaps thought to conflict with the aims and teaching of the Church, such changes were liable to occur; they do not, however, in any way invalidate the view that a common Germanic stock of rune-names existed, that these names possessed considerable antiquity, and that they were familiar wherever runes were known and used.

---

[1] The *Abecedarium Nordmannicum*, the shortest and oldest of the four runic poems, occurs in an early ninth-century MS. of Hrabanus Maurus; it contains in terse alliterative staves the sixteen names of the reduced Northern fuþark (of which it is the earliest known example) in a curious mixture of Northern, Low German and High German forms. The Norwegian and Icelandic poems are of the twelfth to thirteenth and the fifteenth century respectively. See Dickins, *Runic and Heroic Poems*, and G. Baesecke, 'Das Abecedarium Nordmannicum', *Runenberichte* (1941), pp. 76 ff.

The seemingly haphazard nomenclature of the runes has given rise to many and varied attempts at explanation. Some scholars see in these names little more than mere mnemonic words designed to aid the learning and retention of the fuþark, much in the manner of the A for Able, B for Baker, C for Charlie, and their variants used in signalling and telephone conversations. But a closer analysis of the names and their meanings suggests a deeper significance; it suggests indeed that of the Germanic world of gods and giants, of men and natural forces and treasured possessions many of the most conspicuous features were mirrored in the naming of the runes.[1] To us today these names afford invaluable insight into what was cherished or feared, important in one way or another in the lives of these early communities. Ritual, religion, magic, symbolical associations of various kinds cling to most of the names, and their echoes can still be heard in the much later runic poems and even in the thoroughly Christian verse of the ninth-century poet Cynewulf; in Scandinavia these echoes persist even longer. That is why any simple classification according to the literal meaning of the rune-names is inevitably insufficient, perhaps even misleading. It will be worth while examining a few instances in some detail.

Thus Gc. *berkana-, for instance, literally 'birch twig', is undoubtedly to be connected with fertility cults, symbolising the awakening of nature in spring and the birth of new life generally. In many parts of Europe the birch has long played a role in popular beliefs and customs going back beyond Christianity. To promote fruitfulness among men and beasts birch saplings were placed in houses and stables, and young men and women as well as cattle were struck with birch twigs.[2] In England there existed an old Cheshire custom of fixing a birch twig over the sweetheart's door on May Day, and there is the traditional

---

[1] The most recent detailed study of the rune-names along these lines (which reached me too late for critical consideration in this chapter) is K. Schneider, *Die germanischen Runennamen. Versuch einer Gesamtdeutung* (Meisenheim am Glan, 1956).

[2] W. Mannhardt, *Der Baumkultus der Germanen und ihrer Nachbarstämme*, vol. I (1875), pp. 160 f., 298.

Germanic Runes Names	Old English Runes Names	Abeced. Nord. Runes Names	ON Runes	Pr. ON Names	Norweg. Rune Poem	Icel. Rune Poem	Gothic Runes	Gothic Rune- Letter Names	Gothic Letter Names	Gothic Letters
*fёhu	feoh	feu		*fehu	fé	fé		*falhu	fe	
*úruz	úr	úr		*úruR	úr	úr		*urus	uraz	
*þurisaz	þorn	thuris		*þurisaR	þurs	þurs		*paúris	thyth	
*ansuz	ōs	ōs		*ą́suR	óss	óss		*ansus	aza	
*raidō	rād	rāt		*raiðu	reið	reið		*raida	reda	
*kaunaz / *kēnaz / *kanō	cēn	chaon		*kauna	kaun	kaun		*kusma	chozma	
*gebō	gyfu			*gebu				*giba	geuua	
*wunjō	wyn			*wunju				*winja	uuinne	
*hagalaz	hægl	hagal		*hagla	hagall	hagall		*hagl	haal	
*nauþiz	nӯd	naut		*nauðiR	nauðr	nauðr		*nauþs	noicz	
*īsa-	īs	īs		*isaR	ís	ís		*eis	iiz	
*jēra-	gēr	ār		*jára	ár	ár		*jēr	gaar	
*eihwaz	ēoh			*ihwaR				*aíhus	uuaer	
*perþ-	peorð			*perþru				*paírþra	pertra	
*algiz	eolh (secg)	ӯr		*algiR	ӯr	ӯr		*algs	ezec	

Table V. Rune-names.

*sowelu	sigel	sol	*sowelu	sól	sól	*saúil	sugil
*teiwaz	tir	tiu	*tiwaR	týr	týr	*teiws	tyz
*berkana-	beorc	brica	*berkana	bjarkan	bjarkan	*baírkan	bercna
*chwaz	e(o)h		*ehwaR			*ēgeis	eyz
*mannaz	man	man	*mannaR	maðr	maðr	*manna	manna
*laguz	lagu	lagu	*laguR	lǫgr	lögr	*lagus	laaz
*inguz	Ing		*IngwaR			*Iggws	enguz
*ōþila	ēþel		*óþala			*óþal	utal
*dagaz	dæg		*dagaR			*dags	daaz
	āc						
	æsc						
	ȳr						
	ear						
	ior						
	calc						
	gār						
	cweorð						*qaírþra	quertra
	stān						

association with rebirth in the familiar lines from *The Wife of Usher's Well*:

> The carlin wife's three sons came hame,
> And their hats were o the birk...
> But at the gates o Paradise
> That birk grew fair eneugh.

Such traditions underline the symbolism of the birch and help to account for its choice as a rune-name.

Gc. *$\bar{u}ruz$ is literally 'aurochs' (*bos primigenius*), a species of wild ox found in many parts of Europe until the eleventh century and in some until much later. We cannot be quite sure why this word came to be adopted into the naming of the fuþark, but there are several possible explanations. One is that the animal was used for sacrifices such as were frequently offered to their gods by all the pagan Germanic peoples whether in private or in great shrines like that of Freyr at Uppsala or such as is described in some detail in the *Eyrbyggja Saga*. The *urus* may thus in some way have come to be regarded almost as a sacred animal. On the other hand, an even more plausible suggestion is this: we have evidence that the hunting and slaying of the *urus* was almost a ritual among the Germani and that great fame derived from it. The passage in Caesar's *Gallic War* is worth quoting in full:

A third species [of rare animals] is that which they call aurochs. These are somewhat smaller in size than elephants, and are like bulls in appearance, colour, and shape. Great is their strength and great is their speed,[1] and once they have spied man or beast they do not spare them. These the Germani capture skilfully in pits; and their young men harden themselves by such labour and exercise themselves by this kind of hunting. And those who have slain most of the beasts bring the horns as evidence thereof to a public place and win great fame. The animals, even if caught very young, cannot be tamed or accustomed to human beings. Their horns differ very much from those of our oxen in size and shape and kind. The Germani collect them eagerly, encase their edges in silver, and use them as beakers at their most magnificent banquets.[2]

[1] Pliny, *Natural History*, VIII, 15, makes exactly the same comment about the Germanic *urus*.
[2] *De Bello Gallico*, VI, 28.

The suggestion has been put forward[1] that the name *ūruz symbolises 'manly strength', a concept suggested by the phallic appearance of the rune itself as much as by the strength of the animal. The objection to this view has been well stated by the late Fernand Mossé:[2] 'Granted that the wild ox is a fit representative of brute force, I do not see why it should be equated with man.' Caesar's passage, however, throws a different light on this suggestion, for the urus provided young men with a trial of *their* strength and the word thus undoubtedly suggested concepts of manly strength, of valiant achievement and renown—enough to qualify it amply for inclusion in the fuþark. That the meaning 'manly strength' fits admirably into the Cynewulfian runic passages does not constitute primary evidence, but it is a supporting argument worth keeping in mind.[3]

*jēra, 'year', signifies not just the whole year but especially 'harvest', the most vital season of the year in any agricultural community; and so on with other rune-names, as we shall see below.

The two names O.E. peorþ and cweorþ, like the corresponding Gothic letter-names pertra and quertra, have thus far defied satisfactory explanation. As the q-rune was a late addition prompted by the Latin alphabet, the Old English name cweorþ is probably only a meaningless rhyme to peorþ on which it follows in the sequence of the Latin alphabet. The Gothic quertra may be explained in the same way. The name peorþ represents a Germanic root *perþ-, possibly derived from a foreign source, perhaps Celtic; initial p- was rare in Germanic and no native word significant enough for a rune-name may have begun with this sound. In any case, it remains a puzzle to this day.[4]

Another difficult and much discussed name is that of the rune ᛉ z which represents a sound not found initially at all in

---

[1] Krause, *Runeninschriften im Älteren Futhark*, p. 59; Arntz, *Handbuch*[2], p. 189.

[2] In a personal letter of 2 February 1954.

[3] See my articles on Cynewulf's runes in *English Studies*, vol. 34 (1953), pp. 49ff., 193ff.

[4] For a new attempt at interpreting these two names, see Schneider, *op. cit.* pp. 142ff., 411ff.

Germanic, hence the original namer had an unusual freedom of choice. In Scandinavian usage this rune, commonly ᛅ, acquired the name of the ᛦ rune with the more specific meaning of 'a bow made of yew wood'. In Old English all we have is the problematic *eolhx* of the *Runic Poem* in a stanza suggesting a reference to some species of water reed. The Old English word *eolh*, however, means 'elk', and working back, as it were, from this to the Germanic root we obtain the possible alternatives **alhiz* and **algiz*. Both these have been explored in attempts to establish the original form and meaning of this rune-name. The more fanciful school believes that the rune was named **alhiz*, 'elk', in honour of the rather obscure divinities mentioned as Alcis by Tacitus[1] and there said to have been worshipped as brothers and young men by an equally obscure Germanic tribe. But Tacitus adds that the Alcis have no images, *nulla simulacra*, which seems to preclude elks as well, and Caesar's reference to elks (*alces*) makes no mention of anything non-zoological.[2] In any case it seems unlikely that the namer of the fuþark, with half the word-hoard of his language at his disposal in this case, would have picked an obscure divinity for inclusion in a list so largely practical—an objection which certainly does not apply to the other divinities included in the fuþark.

More straightforward is the assumption that *eolhx* in the *Runic Poem* stands for *eolh-secg*, some sort of sedge or rush,[3] possibly even the Latin *helix*,[4] some 'twisted plant' or 'willow'. Such a reading makes sense of the stanza in the poem, especially as earlier forms of this word found in some Old English glosses (*eolxsecg*, *eolugsecg*, *ilugsegg*, *ilugseg*, all glossed *papiluus*, ?'papyrus') rule out any connection with elks.[5] But all this does not get us any nearer to the original name of the rune. However, the rune ᛦ had become superfluous in Old English and its place in most of the manuscript fuþorcs is taken by Latin *x*.

[1] *Germania*, ch. 43.   [2] *De Bello Gallico*, v, 27.
[3] This has been the most common interpretation since the time of Grimm (*Über deutsche Runen* (1821), p. 221). Cf. E. v. K. Dobbie, *The Anglo-Saxon Minor Poems* (New York, 1942), pp. 156 f.
[4] W. J. Redbond, *Mod. Lang. Review*, vol. 31 (1936), pp. 55 ff.
[5] Cf. Dickins, *Runic and Heroic Poems*, p. 17.

Due to this change the traditional name had probably become corrupt and misunderstood until it appears as *eolhx* in the poem, as *ilcs* in the Vienna codex, besides other even less intelligible variants all ending in *x* in later manuscript fuþorcs: *iolx, ilx, ilix, elux, elox*.[1] Of these only the form *eolh-x* can help us because it can take us back to a Germanic **algiz*, the most likely name of this rune with the meaning 'protection, defence'.[2] It is a good name for two reasons: in the first place it describes in a word the picture of the outstretched fingers suggested by the symbol—the instinctive protective gesture of children or primitive (and not so primitive) people in a moment of fear, as it appears drawn on the sixth-century runic stone of Krogsta (Uppland, Sweden).[3] And secondly, this rune follows almost at once and in the Kylver fuþark immediately after the 'yew' rune with its magical associations.[4] Moreover, it is worth recalling that the Old English *Runic Poem* preserves most of the older rune-names well, and allowing for corruption, possible Christian influence, and even some sort of popular etymology, the form it gives of this name is not very far removed from the original. If *algiz* then was the original name of the *z*-rune it would again help to emphasise the deeper, yet often quite immediate, personal significance of the rune-names.

Two other disputed rune-names belong to the Old English fuþorc only: *ear* and *ior*, the names respectively of the runes ᛠ *êa* and ᛡ *io*. The Old English *Runic Poem* devotes the two final stanzas to these runes although reversing what would be their more correct order: ᛠ *êa* belongs to the first extension of the fuþark, but in the poem is made the subject of the final stanza. It so happens that *ear* is an ordinary Anglo-Saxon noun with two meanings: (1) 'ocean, sea, wave'; (2) 'earth, soil,

---

[1] Cf. Derolez, *Runica Manuscripta*, chs. I and II. In the runic alphabets the name *(b)elach* and its variants probably represent an Old High German version of O.E. *eolh*; *ibid.* p. 370.

[2] Cf. O.E. *ealgian*, 'to protect, defend'; probably O.E. *ealh*, 'temple' is also related. Cf. the Greek cognate ἀλκή, 'strength, warding off'.

[3] Cf. Bugge and Olsen, *Norges Indskrifter med de ældre Runer*, vol. I (1891), pp. 128ff.; Krause, *Beiträge zur Runenforschung* (1932), p. 70 and pl. IV.

[4] This rune stands in the middle of the seven magic runes that accompany the drawing of the Krogsta stone.

'gravel'.[1] *Ior*, on the other hand, is merely a meaningless development of the early Scandinavian *jár, 'year', thus duplicating the
name of the twelfth rune, O.E. *gēr*, 'year, harvest', from the same
source.[2] In the *Runic Poem*, according to our only extant version,
the text printed by Hickes in 1705, *ior* appears as *iar* which is
phonetically very close to the name *ear*, and it seems to me that
the poet overcame the difficulty of the meaningless *ior* (or *iar*)
by simply attaching to it the first of the two meanings of *ear*,
namely 'ocean, sea'. The stanza in the *Runic Poem* makes quite
acceptable sense when thus interpreted. In the final stanza *ear*
itself is used in the sense of 'earth, soil' with specific reference
to the grave, thus concluding the poem in a fitting manner.

Despite this nonce usage in the *Runic Poem*, however, I believe
that normally *ear*, when functioning as a rune-name, means
'ocean, sea', the more common meaning of the word in Anglo-
Saxon usage. Most of the additional Anglo-Saxon runes were
given names that were part of the ordinary vocabulary of Old
English, and, in the Anglo-Saxon poem *The Husband's Message*,
ear occurs as part of the runic cypher with the likely meaning of
'sea'.[3]

The remaining rune-names are less problematic, although in
some cases their full significance may be difficult for us to
recapture. Broadly speaking, however, we can classify them
according to their primary associations with the world of
Germanic gods and giants, with various aspects of nature, or
with the lives and activities of men.

THE WORLD OF GODS

Gc. *þurisaz, 'giant', 'demon', replaced in Old English by
þorn, 'thorn', possibly suggested by the shape of the rune Þ.
Giants were commonly believed in throughout the Germanic

[1] The first meaning occurs in Old English poetry and poetic compounds like
eargrund (*Azarias*, 40). The second meaning occurs in the place-names Earith
(Hunts), Erith (Kent), Yarmouth (Isle of Wight); cf. English Place-Name
Society, vol. 3, pp. xvii, 204 f.; vol. 25, pp. 143 f.

[2] Cf. above, p. 37.

[3] The traditional interpretation of *ior* in the *Runic Poem* as some kind of amphi-
bious creature or else an eel is based on the emendation of the text as handed
down by Hickes. Cf. *J. Engl. and Germanic Philol.* vol. 54 (1955), pp. 1 ff.

world and figure frequently in Scandinavian literature, for instance the eddic *Skírnismál*, where, in stanza 36, reference is made to the scratching of a *þ*-rune,

> þurs ríst ek þér ok þriá stafi.

The two Scandinavian rune-poems refer to giants as 'torturers of women'; the Icelandic poem continues 'and cliff-dweller and husband of a giantess'.[1] Echoes of giant-lore live on in Anglo-Saxon literature.

Gc. *ansuz*, 'god', retained in the Icelandic runic poem and glossed 'prince of Asgard and lord of Valhalla',[2] but replaced in the Old English poem by homonymous Latin *ōs*, 'mouth',[3] and in the Norwegian poem by *óss*, 'mouth of a river'.

Gc. *teiwaz*, the god Tíw, O.N. Týr, as in O.E. *Tíwesdæg*, 'Tuesday'. The name was often invoked as an aid to victory in battle with the aid of the rune; on the Lindholm amulet this and the *ansuz* rune figure several times. The Old English form of the name in the *Runic Poem*, *tír*, suggests Scandinavian influence, while the verse itself appears to refer to some constellation.

Gc. *inguz*, the god Ing, the eponymous hero of the *Ingwine*, a name applied to the Danes in *Beowulf*, 1044, 1319, and generally equated with the Ingaevones of Tacitus.[4] The old tradition of the name is quite clearly retained in the Old English poem.

THE WORLD OF NATURE

Gc. *ūruz*, 'aurochs', 'manly strength': this has already been discussed above.

Gc. *hagalaz*, 'hail', and Gc. *ísa-*, 'ice', interpreted quite literally in the runic poems, were clearly associated with damaging natural forces.

Gc. *eihwaz*, 'yew', the *éoh* of the Old English poem, is etymologically the same word as the rune-name *ýr*, 'bow made of yew'. Yew was closely associated with rune-magic; four of the extant Frisian runic finds are made of yew wood, which was not

---

[1] Dickins, *Runic and Heroic Poems*, p. 29.   [2] *Ibid.*
[3] Thus also Dickins, p. 13, although he suggests elsewhere that the word here refers to Woden.   [4] *Germania*, ch. 2.

only very hard and durable (hence its common use for bows), but also credited with specific avertive powers.[1]

Gc. *sōwelu, 'sun', corresponds to O.N. *sól*; O.E. *sigel* has the same meaning but is of different etymology. Apart from Caesar's reference[2] there is direct evidence of sun-worship among Germanic peoples, notably in the recurrent circle and swastika motifs of the rock-drawings (cf. Text-fig. 2, p. 64). The sun-wagon of Trundholm in Zealand, of the early Bronze Age, links sun and horse,[3] so that the rune-name Gc. *ehwaz, 'horse', the *eh* of the Old English poem, may be linked to the name 'sun' by symbolising the course of the sun. The horse is said by Tacitus to have been a sacred animal in Germania, and the actions and neighing of sacred horses were studiously observed in priestly and royal divination.[4] 'Sun' and 'horse' may thus have been closely connected in original runic nomenclature, and even as the earlier symbolism faded there remained the importance of the sun as the source of warmth and health and fruitfulness, while the horse remained, if not sacred, exceedingly treasured. In the poignant *ubi sunt?* passage of *The Wanderer* the horse stands first: 'hwær cwom mearg?', 'Whither has gone the horse?', and in the *Runic Poem* it is 'unstyllum æfre frofor', 'ever a comfort to the restless'.

Gc. *berkana-, 'birch twig', is clearly to be associated with fertility cults, as we have already seen above. In the Old English poem the whole tree is meant, although the description there given is more easily applied to the poplar than to the birch.[5]

Gc. *laguz, 'water': this may represent water as a source of fertility, or else may be associated with the nether water-realms of early Germanic cosmology, the abode of demons and monsters like those inhabiting Grendel's mere in *Beowulf*, or with ship-burials as in the opening passage of that poem.[6]

---

[1] For the connection between yew-lore and rune-lore, see my study, 'Runes, Yews, and Magic', *Speculum, loc. cit.*   [2] *De Bello Gallico*, VI, 21.

[3] H. Shetelig and H. Falk, *Scandinavian Archaeology*, trans. E. V. Gordon (Oxford, 1937), p. 156, pl. 25.

[4] *Germania*, ch. 10. On the place of the horse in rune-magic, see also Krause, *Beiträge zur Runenforschung* (1932), pp. 65 ff.

[5] Dickins, *Runic and Heroic Poems*, pp. 18 f.

[6] Thus Schneider, *op. cit.* pp. 83 ff.

Gc. *đagaz, 'day', symbolises light, prosperity, fruitfulness; its connection with *sowelu and the sun-cult is obvious. 'Day', moreover, meant security in a world where darkness had, as early Germanic literature shows, many real terrors.

O.E. āc, 'oak', æsc, 'ash', and stān, 'stone', are all late additions to the stock of traditional rune-names due to the Anglo-Saxon extension of the older fuþark. They all derive from the common Old English vocabulary. In the Runic Poem the first refers both to an acorn and to a ship built of oak, the second to the tree and to an ashen spear.

THE WORLD OF MAN

Gc. *fehu, 'cattle', the first name of the fuþark, represents a vital aspect of the life of any agricultural community.

Gc. *raiđō, 'riding, journey', is perhaps to be associated with the belief that after death the soul had to take a long journey. We possess visible proof of this belief in the Sutton Hoo ship burial,[1] paralleled in Old English verse by the opening section of Beowulf. Thus interpreted the r-rune could conceivably have come to function almost as a journey-charm, whether for the living or for the dead. In the three runic poems the word 'riding' is interpreted quite literally.

Gc. *kaunaz, 'ulcer', or *kēnaz, 'torch': here our sources differ. The Scandinavian forms (kaun in both poems) indicate the former; the Old English poem and Cynewulf's usage the latter. Another suggestion put forward[2] is that the original name was *kanō, 'skiff', associated with the cult of the goddess Nerthus.[3] Again, it seems to me safest to trust the English Runic Poem in our search for a solution. 'Torch' could be a symbol of fire, as it is in Cynewulf's runic passage in Christ II, linked with the sun-cult, gradually coming to symbolise the security and comfort of the torch-lit hall, as the Runic Poem suggests. Schneider associates this name with cremation.[4]

[1] See especially The Sutton Hoo Ship Burial. A Provisional Guide, published by the British Museum (London, 1951).
[2] W. Jungandreas, 'Die germanische Runenreihe und ihre Bedeutung', Z. deut. Philol. vol. 60 (1935), pp. 105 ff.
[3] Cf. Tacitus, Germania, ch. 40, and Chadwick, The Origin of the English Nation (Cambridge, 1907), ch. X.   [4] Schneider, op. cit. pp. 74 ff.

Gc. *geƀō, 'gift', may originally have denoted gifts or sacrifices offered to the gods, or possibly gifts received from the gods by men. Gifts presented by a chief to trusty and loyal followers figure prominently in early Germanic literature.

Gc. *wunjō, 'joy': this meaning persists in the Old English poem and in Cynewulf's runic passages. Possible original connections with Gc. *wulþuz, 'glory', and the god Ullr, or else with Gc. *winjō, 'pasture', have also been suggested.[1] But 'joy' was a concrete enough concept to the Germanic man or woman: it probably included, as in the Old English runic stanza, concrete possessions as well as the absence of 'suffering, hardship and sorrow'—again a suitable word for the rune-magic of the fuþark.

Gc. *nauþiz, 'need, necessity, constraint', is perhaps to be connected with the rune-names 'hail' and 'ice' which enclose it in the traditional sequence of the fuþark and which are the direct causes of such human plight. All three contrast sharply with *jēra-, the name that immediately follows.

Gc. *jēra-, 'year', 'the fertile season, harvest', was yet another vital concept in any primitive agricultural community. Later the word came to mean 'year', but the older harvest association is still echoed in the *Runic Poem* which mentions fruits in this connection.

Gc. *algiz, 'defence, protection', a name already discussed above.

Gc. *mannaz, 'man', may refer either literally to the race of men or perhaps symbolise the legendary progenitor of the human race; cf. Tacitus, *Germania*, ch. 2.

Gc. *ōþila or *ōþala, 'inherited possession or property', is the last of the original twenty-four rune-names; possibly it means more specifically 'land', as in later usage, thus complementing the movable property implied by the first rune-name, *fehu, 'cattle'.

O.E. ȳr, 'bow made of yew wood', is etymologically the same as the rune-name ēoh, Gc. *eihwaz, 'yew'; it was probably adopted into Old English from Scandinavian sources as the

[1] Cf. Arntz, *Handbuch*[2], pp. 203 f.

name for one of the additional runes of the Anglo-Saxon fuþorc. Yew-bows were cherished throughout Europe for the hard and durable quality of the wood: the hunting-god Ullr appropriately built his hall in Ýdalir, the valley of the yews,[1] and there is similar evidence in classical literature and in English from the Middle Ages to Conan Doyle's *Song of the Bow*.

O.E. *calc* and *gār* are also later English additions due to the final extension of the fuþorc in Northumbria. The latter certainly means 'spear', the former may be 'sandal, shoe' (from Latin *calceus*), or 'chalice, beaker' (from Latin *calix*) or a variant of O.E. *cealc* 'chalk'; but as the *Runic Poem* does not help, the meaning of the name must remain speculative.

The sequence of the twenty-four runes of the common Germanic fuþark was most likely determined in the main by the North Italic prototype, although modifications, including the insertion of new symbols in certain places, must have taken place. The order of the rune-names was thus largely predetermined. The latter were, however, Germanic creations, for there is no evidence to suggest that the Italic letters had names.

Although the order of the rune-names was thus in some measure fortuitous, the choice of names clearly was not; and while the ultimate significance of certain names may yet elude us and make any classification merely tentative, the majority point unmistakably to aspects of early Germanic life and to various cults and religious beliefs. On the other hand it is obvious that the choice of names was severely restricted: each rune could possess but one name; that name had to begin with the given sound; and where several suitable words qualified for inclusion only one, presumably the most significant, could be chosen. In other cases words of less immediate significance may have had to be adopted for want of better alternatives.

Some scholars have tried to connect the names with the shapes of certain runes, but it is difficult to believe that such connection exists, except possibly quite accidentally. The only instances where the shape of a rune may well have suggested its

[1] *Grímnismál*, 5.

name are ᛉ *algiz*, 'protection', the outstretched fingers of the hand, and O.E. *þorn*, 'thorn', for ᚦ, but this latter is a later renaming; the original Germanic name **þurisaz* cannot have been inspired by the shape of the rune.

Yet within the arbitrary sequence of the rune-names a few connected groups do seem to occur, if our interpretations are correct. Such groups are especially: 'sun', the focal point of early Germanic religious belief; 'Týr', the old sky-god; 'birch-twig', the symbol of fertility; 'horse', that which guides the sun across its path; 'man', the symbol of mankind or of its deified progenitor; 'water', source of fertility; 'Ing', venerated as the god of fertility with whose cult the Ingaevones are associated. Another group, already alluded to, is that dealing with hostile natural forces and their resulting human 'need': 'hail', 'need, constraint', 'ice', enclosed, as it were, by the contrasting 'gift' and 'joy', and 'harvest'.

Such groupings may be accidental; on the other hand there may well have been some deliberate modifications of the sequence of symbols originally adopted, in order to place certain vital, related concepts together. At our present state of knowledge no final solution can be offered.

What we may, however, regard as certain is the ritual import of the rune-names which the present chapter has tried to elucidate. No other explanation can account for the obviously meaningful use of single or multiplied runes like those of the Lindholm amulet (*aaaaaaaaRRRnnn...bmutt*), the Swedish stone of Gummarp (Blekinge, Sweden, seventh century) (*fff*), and others.[1] Runes were thus used to evoke or protect against the power contained in their names: appeals to the gods, 'prayers' for fertility, for good harvest, for protection against damaging forces, and so forth. The original reason for adopting the North Italic letters may well have been the practice of casting lots, of inscribing pieces of wood with signs, the *notae*

---

[1] In this connection might be noted that magic words which occasionally occur in runic inscriptions, like *alu, auja, laukaz*, generally appear written in full or intelligibly shortened, whereas the words denoted by rune-names are represented by the rune alone. Conversely, where single runes occur, they should always be interpreted as standing for their name.

of Tacitus which were undoubtedly runes,[1] to be interpreted according to their names by the priest or other initiated person. But the naming of the runes in such a significant manner was bound to place them at the very heart of Germanic rite and religion. It is this ritual and religious function more than anything primarily utilitarian which is the foremost characteristic of runic writing.

[1] See below, p. 65.

CHAPTER VI

THE USES OF RUNES

*Runes and charms are very practical formulae designed to
produce definite results, such as getting a cow out of a bog.*
T. S. ELIOT, *The Music of Poetry*

THE primary characteristic of runes, referred to at the close of
the preceding chapter and already apparent from our brief
study of their names, is the important part they played in the
realms of Germanic ritual and magic. Runic writing did not
lend itself readily to the practical uses which we associate with
most forms of alphabetic writing; it never developed into a
cursive script, but remained epigraphic to the end. For the
continuity of tradition in law and legend, in poetry and ritual,
the earlier Germanic peoples depended upon oral transmission.
There are, it is true, occasional saga references to the use of
runes for inscribing poems on pieces of wood,[1] but we may
regard these as exceptions; they belong to a period already
influenced by the use of Latin script. The fragments of the Old
English poem, *The Dream of the Rood*, carved on the Ruthwell
Cross suggest an ornamental purpose rather than a recording
for the sake of literary transmission. Not the fuþark but the
several continental and insular forms of Latin minuscule hand-
writing were adopted in due course for literary and legal recording. Individual runes, as we have seen, found their way into
manuscripts, but it is not until the fourteenth century that we
find a proper runic manuscript codex; and by this time a mixture
of archaic dignity and antiquarian interest would attach to runic
writing in a medieval scriptorium. The manuscript referred to
is the so-called Codex Runicus in Copenhagen which contains,
besides various shorter pieces and fragments, the *Skanske Lov* or

---

[1] For example, in *Egils Saga* and *Grettis Saga*. The 'pieces of wood' are known
technically as O.N. (*rúna*)*kefli* from Gc. **kaƀlja*. Cf., for example, 'Gísli hafði
kefli ok reist á rúnar, ok falla niðr spænirnir', 'Gisli had a rune-staff and cut runes
thereon, and the shavings fell to the ground' (*Gísla Saga*, 67).

provincial law of Skåne (Text-fig. 1). Two later and corrupt versions of the same codex also exist, and there are two further Danish runic manuscripts of the fourteenth and fifteenth centuries respectively. This is a meagre list even when allowance is made for possible runic manuscripts no longer extant; yet it confirms the view that runic writing was neither suited nor primarily intended or employed for practical or literary purposes. Even where its use is mainly utilitarian, in occasional messages and tomb inscriptions for example, there generally clings to it something of the older Germanic rune-lore.

Text-fig. 1. Fragment from the Codex Runicus.

The magic significance attaching to the fuþark was not derived from the North Italic source of the runic letters themselves. Two streams clearly meet in the common Germanic fuþark: on the one hand the signs themselves with their individual shapes and phonetic values point to an affinity with the Alpine alphabets; on the other hand the deeper content and the highly significant names of the runes point unmistakably into the veiled centuries of unrecorded Germanic prehistory. During these centuries, and prior to the adoption of the fuþark, the Germanic peoples possessed no script; they made use, however, of pictorial symbols of various designs scratched into rock and thus technically known as *hällristningar*, 'rock-carvings' (Text-fig. 2).[1] Such picture symbols, particularly

[1] Cf. L. Baltzer, *Hällristningar fran Bohuslän* (Göteborg, 1881–1908) and Shetelig-Falk, *op. cit.* ch. x.

common in Sweden, can be assigned to various prehistoric periods, the greatest number to the second Bronze Age (*c.* 1300 to 1200 B.C.) and the transition to the Iron Age (*c.* 800 to 600 B.C.), but theirs was probably a continuing tradition which finds its origin in the Indo-European sun-cult, and which extends well into our own era. The sun motif which lies at their root is apparent in the many variations of circles, semicircles, swastikas, and the like, but there also occur pictorial representations of men and animals, parts of the human body, and various

Text-fig. 2. *Hällristningar,* 'rock-carvings'.

implements such as axes, arrows, and ships. This rich variety of material constituted no written language but rather points unmistakably to primitive religious beliefs, to fertility and other cults; it also suggests a gradual development towards the mere ornamentation of later designs on Germanic pottery, domestic tools, and weapons.[1]

It was a people with a long tradition in the use and meaning of such pre-runic symbols that the fuþark eventually reached. The result was a gradual amalgamation of the two distinct streams: the alphabetic script on the one hand, the symbolic content on the other. The fusion was made easier because both systems

[1] Arntz, *Handbuch*[2], pp. 125 ff.; Krause, *Runeninschriften im Älteren Futhark,* pp. 427 f.

shared some common ground, not only the formal resemblance of certain signs, such as ↑, ᚺ, ᛁ, ✕, ᛉ, ᚥ, but more especially the use of individual signs for purposes of casting lots and divination. The practice of sortilege was cultivated among Northern Italic as well as Germanic peoples, the one using letters, the others pictorial symbols. There are references to the Germanic practice in Plutarch[1] and Julius Caesar,[2] but our most explicit testimony is that of Tacitus who writes in A.D. 98 (*Germania*, ch. x):

> Auspicia sortesque ut qui maxime observant. Sortium consuetudo simplex: virgam frugiferae arbori decisam in surculos amputant eosque notis quibusdam discretos super candidam vestem temere ac fortuito spargunt; mox, si publice consultetur, sacerdos civitatis, sin privatim, ipse pater familiae precatus deos caelumque suspiciens ter singulos tollit, sublatos secundum impressam ante notam interpretatur.

To divination and lots they pay attention beyond any other people. Their method of casting lots is a simple one: they cut a bough from a fruit-bearing tree and divide it into small pieces; these they mark with certain distinguishing signs and scatter at random and without order over a white cloth. Then, after invoking the gods and with eyes lifted up to heaven, the priest of the community, if the lots are consulted publicly, or, if privately, the father of the family, takes up three pieces one at a time and interprets them according to the signs previously marked on them.

The memory of the Germanic custom lingers in the eddic *Vǫluspá* (st. 20) and in the words *hæl sceawedon*, 'they observed the omens', before Beowulf sailed for Denmark (*Beowulf*, 204); Bede refers to the casting of lots in the *Ecclesiastical History* (Bk. v, ch. 10) as customary among the *Antiqui Saxones*, as does the poet of the Old English *Andreas* (1099 ff.) with his specific mention of heathen practices:

> Leton him þa betweonum taan wisian
> hwylcne hira ærest oðrum sceolde
> to foddurþege feores ongyldan;
> hluton hellcræftum, hæðengildum
> teledon betwinum.

---

[1] *Marius*, 15, 4; I am interpreting the passage quite literally.
[2] *De Bello Gallico*, 1, 50. Caesar here ascribes the Germanic custom of casting lots and divination to the *matres familiae*.

Casting lots they let them decree
Which should die first as food for the others.
With hellish acts and heathen rites
They cast the lots and counted them out.[1]

Tacitus makes the procedure quite clear but does not specify the *notae* which were thus scratched into pieces of wood. Undoubtedly by his time they were runes. The fusion I have suggested made the fuþark heir to the symbolic content of the earlier rock-pictures; individual runes came to be used for sortilege, their names pointing to the required interpretation. Here then is the bridge which links the two systems. For a time they co-existed: pre-runic picture-symbols appear side by side with runes in early runic inscriptions, for example on the rocks of Kårstad (Nordfjord, Norway) and Himmelstadlund (Östergötland, Sweden),[2] and on the third-century spearhead found near Kowel (south of Brest-Litovsk, near the present Russo-Polish frontier).[3] We cannot determine for certain whether the picture-symbols here still possessed a live significance; they may already have become largely ornamental, especially on the Kowel spearhead. But there can be little doubt that their earlier magico-religious function had been inherited by the fuþark by the time of Tacitus.

The word 'rune' itself places the fuþark at the very heart of Germanic religious cult; to this day the German *raunen* connotes 'whisper' and 'secret' and 'mystery', associations coeval with the powerful magic of runic lore. Nor is evidence lacking to connect the secrets of runes with the Germanic gods themselves. In the eddic *Hávamál* Woden, the 'High One', describes the passion and self-sacrifice which led him to the knowledge and wisdom of the runes (st. 138 f.). For nine nights Woden hung upon the world-ash Yggdrasil, wounded by his own weapon, tormented by pain, hunger, and thirst, until at last he spied the runes and with tremendous effort grasped them ere he

---

[1] Translated by C. W. Kennedy, *Early English Christian Poetry* (London, 1952).
[2] Krause, *op. cit.* pp. 492 ff.
[3] *Ibid.* pp. 441 f.; Arntz–Zeiss, *op. cit.* pp. 19 ff. and plate 2.

fell. And now the god throve and grew in wisdom, he became god of rune-lore and magic as of eloquence and poetry. From Woden the secrets of runic wisdom passed to men and with them the firm belief in the magic efficacy of the complete fuþark and its separate runes. Both good and evil could be effected by their skilful use. A famous passage interpolated in the eddic *Sigrdrífumál* enumerates victory-runes, ale-runes,[1] birth-runes, surf-runes,[2] health-runes, speech-runes, thought-runes. Fertility and love-runes, battle-runes[3] and weather-runes may be added from other sources. The *Hávamál* (st. 157) credits runes with the power of resurrecting the dead:

> þat kann ek it tólpta: ef ek sé á tré uppi
> váfa virgilná,
> sva ek ríst ok í rúnom fák,
> at sá gengr gumi
> ok mælir við mik.

> A twelfth (spell) I know: when I see aloft upon a tree
> A corpse swinging from a rope,
> Then I cut and paint runes
> So that the man walks
> And speaks with me.

Bede relates (*Hist. Eccl.* bk. IV, ch. 22) how in the year 679 a young Northumbrian captive called Imma whose fetters fell off whenever his brother, believing him dead, celebrated mass for the delivery of his soul, was asked whether he carried on him *litteras solutorias*. The Old English version reads: 'hwæðer he þa alysendlecan rune cuðe and þa stafas mid him awritene hæfde', 'whether he knew loosening runes and had about him the letters written down', a clear testimony that the belief in the magical efficacy of runes was then still very much alive.

[1] Traditionally so regarded, but more probably the falling together of Gc. **aluþ*, 'ale', with the magic avertive formula *alu*, 'taboo', in primitive Old Norse caused misunderstanding, for the latter is the more likely meaning here.

[2] The yew-wand of Westeremden (Fig. 22), which incidentally appears to contain a reference to Hamlet (*Amluþ*), records the power of its runes over the waves.

[3] The Britsum amulet inscription (Fig. 21) has been interpreted as 'always carry this yew in the host of battle' (W. J. Buma, 'Das Runenstäbchen von Britsum', *Beiträge z. Gesch. deut. Sprache und Literatur*, vol. 73 (1951), pp. 306ff.). Other amulets, like Lindholm (Fig. 19) or Wijnaldum (Fig. 20), may have been carried about for less specific purposes.

Embued with powers such as these it is no wonder that runes were readily scratched for many a specific purpose on to a variety of objects, many of them ephemeral like wooden staffs or twigs and thus long since decayed. These inscriptions took various forms according to the effect desired: single runes credited with particular powers, such as ↑ *t* (*Týr*) for victory in battle; series of separate runes, single or multiplied as on the Lindholm amulet; magic words like *alu*, 'protection, taboo', or *laukaz*, 'leek'; whole fuþarks as on the Vadstena and Grumpan bracteates or the Thames scramasax; and finally proper inscriptions such as survive on stones, weapons, and other objects. Among Anglo-Saxon runic remains, for example, are several amulet rings, now in the British Museum, with almost identical but hitherto unexplained inscriptions of undoubted magical significance (Fig. 18).[1]

The scratching of runes on to staffs or objects of various kinds for immediate practical purposes, such as curing a disease,[2] frequently no doubt went hand in hand with the reciting of charms or spells in order to enhance their potency. The *Hávamál* lists eighteen such spells of which the one cited above specifically mentions runes.[3] There are also extant a number of Old English and Old High German charms whose subject-matter places them in close relationship to rune-magic. Woden is mentioned in the Anglo-Saxon *Nine Herbs Charm* and in the second Old High German *Merseburger Zauberspruch*, and there is in several passages clear indication of considerable pagan antiquity, despite later additions of Christian thought and vocabulary:

> þa genam Woden viiii wuldortanas,
> sloh ða þa næddran þæt heo on viiii tofleah,

> For Woden took nine glory-twigs,
> he smote then the adder that it flew apart into nine parts.[4]

---

[1] Cf. B. Dickins, 'Runic Rings and Old English Charms', *Archiv Stud. neueren Sprachen*, vol. 67, n.s. (1935), p. 252.

[2] As in *Egil's Saga*, ch. 72; cf. above, p. 29.

[3] For other examples, see *Sigrdrífumál*, 6 ff., *Grógaldr*, 6 ff., *Vǫlsunga Saga*, ch. 20, and *Grettis Saga*, ch. 81.

[4] G. Storms, *Anglo-Saxon Magic* (The Hague, 1948), pp. 188-9.

'He takes nine glory-twigs, by which are meant nine runes, that is nine twigs with the initial letters in runes of the plants representing the power inherent in them, and using them as weapons he smites the serpent with them. Thanks to their magical power they pierce its skin and cut it into nine pieces.'[1]

Belief in rune-magic survived the spread of Christianity in some places into the later Middle Ages, in Iceland, as we have seen, until the seventeenth century. Although in the story of Imma Bede was primarily concerned with recording a Christian miracle, he furnishes incidentally valuable evidence for the still current belief in rune-magic. An interesting Anglo-Saxon example of ancient runic lore in Christian dress is the poem *Solomon and Saturn*, where the letters making up the Latin *Pater Noster* are accompanied by their corresponding runes in a passage advocating the use of the Lord's Prayer as an effective war-spell in battle. The association of runes and magic, then, lives long: Abbot Ælfric equates runes and magic, in the eleventh century, in one of his sermons: 'ðurh drycræft oððe ðurh runstafum', 'through magic or through runes'.[2] The persistence of superstitions and popular customs involving yew-lore and runic magic, as in popular medicine, should also be remembered in this context.

Reaching from magic to secular usage of runes is their frequent employment on tomb inscriptions. In the Scandinavian countries, it will be recalled, these are particularly common, and there they span the Viking centuries, heathen and Christian. Several categories may be distinguished here:

(1) Inscriptions designed to ward off evil forces or to confine the dead person to his grave: such inscriptions were generally made on stones placed *inside* the grave, which stresses their magical function. The stone of Noleby (Skaraborgs län, Sweden, sixth century; Fig. 28) and the justly famed Eggjum stone (Sogndal, Nordre Bergenhus Amt, Norway, eighth century),[3] belong to this class. The Eggjum stone contains the longest

[1] *Ibid.* p. 195.
[2] *Homilies*, ed. Thorpe, vol. 2, p. 358.
[3] Good plates of this, with earlier literature, can be found in A. Heiermeier, *Der Runenstein von Eggjum* (Halle, 1934).

known inscription in the common Germanic fuþark and throws some interesting light on Germanic burial practices. These inscriptions rarely record the name of the deceased; of much greater significance was the name of the rune-master whose art was here put to such vital use.

(2) Another type of inscription not recording the name of the dead person is found on the Scandinavian *bauta*-stones.[1] These cairn-like stones, rough, unhewn boulders ranging in height from 3 to 18 feet, were generally placed close to a grave. Where runes occur on them they usually contain some reference to the writer which was deemed sufficiently effective to control the dead man or to ward off hostile intruders. One such stone still standing on its original site is that of *Einang* (Kristians Amt, Norway) of the later fourth century; it reads: 'đagaR þaR runo faihiđo', '(I) Dagr painted the runes'.

(3) It was no great step from such inscriptions of a definitely magical nature to others which combined this function with a commemorative one by including the dead person's name, and thence, finally, to memorial inscriptions pure and simple. With this last development, it will be noted, the fuþark loses its main original feature and becomes a purely communicative script. Among inscriptions of the last type are the well-known ones on the stones of Möjbro (Uppsala län, Sweden, fifth century), Tune (Smaalenenes Amt, Norway, fifth century), and Istaby (Blekinge, Sweden, seventh century; Fig. 29). The latter, to cite an example, reads: 'afạtR hariwulạfạ haþuwulạfR haeruwulạfiR wạrait runaR þaiaR', 'After Hariwulf Hathuwulf, Heruwulf's son, wrote these runes'.

(4) A final group of pagan Germanic memorial stones are the numerous stones of the great Viking period, often erected to the memory of men slain far from home. Little, if any, trace of magic now remains and the runic inscriptions, generally approaching formula-like expression, are placed conspicuously for all to see, inscribed in bands which are often artistically intertwined in impressive snake-like patterns.

[1] A Danish word used to describe stones erected in memory of the dead from the Bronze Age onwards.

In England Christianity came too soon to allow the full flowering of runic stone-inscriptions of the kind found throughout the so-called Dark Ages and early Middle Ages in Norway and Sweden and from the ninth century onwards also in Denmark. Nevertheless, runic tomb inscriptions have been found in this country although only the small stone found near Sandwich (Kent; Figs. 26, 27) could possibly be assigned to pagan times.[1] Other runic tomb inscriptions, mainly recovered from Anglo-Saxon cemeteries, often show the name of the deceased person accompanied by a cross. Of this type are two small eighth-century sepulchral stone slabs, known either as 'pillow-stones', or simply as 'name-stones', from Hartlepool (Co. Durham; Fig. 30). In a few cases a pious request for prayer is added as on the biliteral eighth-century stone fragment from Falstone (Northumberland; Fig. 32) which concludes its parallel Roman and runic inscription with the words 'pray for his soul'. Probably this association of a Christian prayer formula with runic writing represents yet another instance of the mingling of older traditions with the Christian faith: there is no way of proving that superstitious beliefs in the efficacy of runes on tombstones (for the dead man's salvation or against his haunting his survivors) still attach to such inscriptions, but it is a possibility. Why else should runes be used in an age that was fully conversant with Celtic or Roman lettering? The dual inscription on the Falstone stone suggests not a linguistic or epigraphic exercise as much as a sound insurance policy. As in the case of the Scandinavian memorials we usually know nothing of the people mentioned in English inscriptions. The Overchurch limestone fragment, for instance (now in the Grosvenor Museum, Chester),[2] records that 'folce arærdon bec(un); biddaþ fo(r)e æþelmun(de)', 'the people erected this monument; pray for Æthelmund', but it does not tell us who this Æthelmund was, although he appears to have been a more important person than those in the more common family-type

---

[1] Bede (*Hist. Eccl.* 1, 15) refers to the heathen memorial to Horsa as still standing somewhere in east Kent at the time he was writing the *History*.

[2] G. F. Browne, 'On a Sculptured Stone with a Runic Inscription in Cheshire', *J. Chester Archaeol. Hist. Soc.* n.s. vol. 3 (1890), pp. 178 ff.

inscription. It is tempting to see this Æthelmund in one of those of that name listed by Searle,[1] but so far no one has succeeded in establishing his identity beyond reasonable doubt.

Although we have seen that the primary and by far the more important function of runic writing was a magico-religious one, secular uses for various purposes are found from early times. Often the boundary between the two is hard to define, for to the more primitive mind the two would often be identical. Mr T. S. Eliot puts it well in the words cited at the head of this chapter, and worth repeating here: 'Runes and charms are very practical formulae designed to produce definite results, such as getting a cow out of a bog', or, we might add, healing a sick woman, as in *Egil's Saga*, or subduing the waves as with the Britsum amulet. When a sword or spear or other weapon bears a name in runes, sometimes inlaid with gold wire thread or coloured blood-red, the idea may well have been to enhance its striking power as well as to mark the name of its maker or owner. The magnificent sword hilt described in *Beowulf*, ll. 1687 ff.,[2] comes to mind again; the Thames scramasax not only bears the whole fuþorc, but also the name *Bêagnoþ*, and among continental Germanic and Scandinavian finds there are many similar instances. In some cases there is little doubt that the name is that of the weapon itself, for the naming of weapons was as common in the heroic age as in the later age of chivalry. Thus the Øvre Stabu spear-head of the third century (Fig. 8) bears the runes ᚱᚨᚢᚾᛁᛉᚨᚠ(ᛉ) *raunija(z)*, 'assayer, tester'; the Kowel spearhead bears the name *tilariďs* which probably means 'attacker'. The maker's name often figures in runes on weapons, ornaments, and other articles. One of the most famous of all runic finds was the fifth-century golden drinking-horn found in 1734 at Gallehus (Schleswig), which was stolen and melted down in 1802, but of which reliable reproductions exist. Its inscription read: 'ek hlewagastiR holtijaR horna tawido', 'I, Hlewagast, Holt's son, made the horn'. Another well-known example of this type of

---

[1] W. G. Searle, *Onomasticon Anglo-Saxonicum* (Cambridge, 1897), pp. 44 ff.
[2] See above, pp. 18f.

inscription is the 'boso wraet runa', 'Boso wrote the runes' of the sixth-century silver fibula of Freilaubersheim (Germany; Fig. 17). An eighth-century Englishman called Hadda similarly perpetuated his name on a bone plate from Derbyshire, perhaps part of a comb or comb-case, which is now in the British Museum (Fig. 25). On bracteates and coins similar inscriptions occur, in the latter case generally the names of kings or of the moneyers. A series of ninth-century Northumbrian coins in the British Museum, for example, has the moneyer's name Wintred either in runes or in Latin characters or a mixture of both.

Runes were also used to convey messages. In the sixth century Venantius Fortunatus wrote to his friend Flavus:

> Barbara fraxineis pingatur runa tabellis,
> quodque papyrus agit, virgula plana valet.

You may also paint barbaric runes on tablets of ash wood; what papyrus achieves a smoothed wooden staff can do as well.

In the literature of the North there are similar references to such usage, *rúnakefli* being generally used. Thus in *Atlamál*, 4, Guðrún *rúnar nam at rísta*, but her warning runes were altered by Vingi the messenger; Kostbera warns her husband, Högni, that there is something wrong with the runes (st. 10–12), but he does not heed her advice and goes to his doom.[1] In the Old English *The Husband's Message* the wood which carries the message speaks in the first person, and the poem concludes with a runic cypher · ᚻ · ᚱ · ᛦ · ᛈ · ᛗ (or ᛗ) ·, that is *s. r. êa. w. d.* (or *m*, the MS. is ambiguous) which represents the message proper itself and conceals in the five rune-names the gist of the whole poem. Somewhat expanded the message may be taken to be: 'Follow the *sun's path* (*sigel-rād*) south across the *ocean* (*ēar*), and ours will be *joy* (*wyn*) and the happiness and prosperity of the *bright day* (*dæg*)', or, if the final rune is ᛗ (which is perhaps more likely): 'Follow the *sun's path* south across the *ocean* to find *joy* with the *man* (*mon*) who is waiting for you.'[2]

[1] For the prose version see *Volsunga Saga*, chs. 33–4.
[2] Elliott, 'The Runes in the Husband's Message', *J. Engl. and Germanic Philol.* vol. 54 (1955), pp. 1 ff.

Of a similar *genre* is the use of runes in the Old English poetic riddles and the signed poems of Cynewulf. In the runic riddles the solution was inserted into the verse with the aid of runes or rune-names, sometimes spelling backwards to enhance the puzzle. In Cynewulf's verse the poet's name was spelt in runes which in three of the poems were fitted singly into the text so that their names formed part of the narrative; in the fourth poem, *Juliana*, the runes occur in three groups, *cyn*, *ewu*, and *lf*, of which the first two spell normal Old English words, meaning 'mankind' and 'sheep' respectively, whereas the third can only be interpreted as standing for the two rune-names, *lagu* and *feoh*, joined into a compound with the contextual meaning '(earth's) flood-bound wealth'. The poet's purpose, as he expressly states, was to request prayer by name to aid his soul to attain salvation.[1]

The use of individual runes for manuscript purposes to fill gaps in the Latin alphabet (especially *þ*), or as a convenient shorthand, has already been mentioned. In the manuscript of the Old High German *Wessobrunner Gebet* the rune ᚷ occurs four times for the syllable *ga*, probably due to Anglo-Saxon scribal influence on the Continent.[2]

Finally, mention must be made of the use of runes for mainly decorative purposes. The runes on the Ruthwell Cross are probably best explained as further ornamentation for this already generously decorated monument; and to this class we can also assign the beautiful eighth-century whalebone casket (the Franks casket; Figs. 42–6), now in the British Museum, with its series of historical carvings depicting Germanic as well as biblical and classical scenes, and its explanatory runic and Roman inscriptions. The decorative quality of runic writing must, in any case, not be underestimated: where picture-symbols and runes meet in rock-carvings or on spearheads the decorative must be added as a third element to the practical and the magical. We have parallels in the use of Christian symbolism,

---

[1] For the most recent discussion of the *Juliana* runes, see *Juliana*, ed. R. Woolf (London, 1955), pp. 8 ff.

[2] On occasional runes in manuscripts see Derolez, *Runica Manuscripta*, ch. v.

the cross, alpha and omega, and so forth on sacred objects. In the Middle Ages Roman letters were occasionally used for decoration of works of craftsmanship in metal, wood, or leather. The later Viking custom of placing runic stone inscriptions into bands interlaced into the most intricate patterns shows similar awareness of the ornamental possibilities of runic writing.

Secular uses of runes persisted to a diminishing extent into modern times, as we have seen in chapters III and IV. Arntz draws attention to the use of runes for a private journal by a Swedish admiral, Mogens Gyldenstjerne, in 1543, and their use as a secret military code by the Swedish general Jacob de la Gardie in the Thirty Years War.[1] Individual runes lived on in merchants' and masons' and hunters' marks and suchlike both in England and on the Continent, in the lot-casting for hides in country parishes,[2] and the primstaves or perpetual calendars of northern country districts.[3] But these are exceptions. It is clear that once the true character of runic lore had ceased to be a vital force among the Germanic peoples, the drawbacks of runic writing as a purely practical medium prevented any effective competition with Roman-derived minuscules as a suitable everyday script.

[1] Arntz, *Handbuch*[2], p. 255.
[2] C. G. Homeyer, *Die Haus- und Hofmarken* (Berlin, 1870).
[3] J. B. Davis, 'Some Account of Runic Calendars and "Staffordshire Clogg" Almanacs', *Archaeologia*, vol. 41 (1867), pp. 453ff.

CHAPTER VII

SOME ENGLISH RUNIC INSCRIPTIONS

On some far northern strand...
Before some fallen Runic stone.

ARNOLD, *Stanzas from the Grande Chartreuse*

IN this chapter I have selected a number of Anglo-Saxon runic inscriptions for the sake of fuller illustration than was possible in the text. Although English runic remains offer considerable variety and include unique works of art like the Ruthwell Cross or the Franks casket, they cannot rival the numbers and in most cases the antiquity of those of other, especially the Scandinavian, countries. Perhaps this is the reason why we do not as yet possess a comprehensive and adequately illustrated edition of all extant runic inscriptions. Such an edition is sorely needed for students and others interested in early English culture. Such works do exist for other countries and are readily accessible, and for this reason I have not included any foreign monuments in this chapter. Moreover, to do more here than give a selection of English runic finds would have exceeded the scope of the present volume: my endeavour is to illustrate not exhaust the subject. For this reason and also for reasons of space my explanatory comments have been kept brief, and bibliographical references are given only where I feel that they might be of immediate use to English readers.

As practically all Anglo-Saxon runic inscriptions are later than the conversion of England to Christianity any attempt at chronological arrangement, in any case very uncertain, would have served little purpose. I have therefore arranged my selection according to the type of object concerned, in this order: (I) coins; (II) weapons; (III) sepulchral stones; (IV) cross fragments; (V) the Ruthwell Cross; (VI) the Franks casket.

I. COINS

The Scanomodu coin. British Museum. Fig. 11.

This is a barbarous copy in gold of a solidus of Honorius; it is not known for certain where it was found.

The runic inscription reads ⟩ʌⲘⲭⲒ𐍈Ⲙ𐍈ⲭ𐍂 *scanomodu*, most probably a person's name. Most unlikely is the interpretation *Scan o modu*, 'Scan owns this mot (i.e. coin or die)' (Stephens), or the attempt to connect the inscription with the Yorkshire place-name Scammonden.

As Honorius died in A.D. 423, the coin could not be much earlier than the middle of the fifth century; probably it is of somewhat later date and may best be assigned to the sixth century. Its closest parallel is a copy of a solidus of Theodosius I (379–95), found at Harlingen (West Friesland) and now in the Leeuwarden Museum (Fig. 12). This bears in runes the name *hada* on the reverse. It has been suggested that both coins originated in Friesland, but on account of the shape of the *a*-rune I regard the Scanomodu coin as English and consequently as the oldest known English runic inscription.

The *s*-rune ⟩ is found in this shape in common Germanic inscriptions of various periods, but its survival in an English inscription suggests a relatively early date; the same applies to ⋈ *d*, and more especially to ⊗ *o* which here still retains its original sound-value *o*. The *c*-rune ⋌, originally only half-size in Germanic usage, has attained full height as on the Frisian bone-piece of Hantum (Fig. 24), but has not yet quite acquired its characteristic Anglo-Saxon shape ⋀. These four runes suggest a transitional phase between the common Germanic fuþark and the Anglo-Saxon twenty-eight-letter fuþorc proper. ⊱ *a* is a common Anglo-Frisian development but has here its regular Old English appearance; its use for a probably original *au* (**skaunu-*), which is paralleled on the Mercian *pada* coins (see below), implies that the separate *ēa*-rune had not yet come into use. The retention, moreover, of final *-u* after a long stem-syllable (later O.E. *mōd*) speaks equally for a comparatively early date.

77

Mercian sceattas. British Museum. Figs. 13 and 14.

The coins in the British Museum bearing in runes the name ᛈᚪᛞᚪ *pada* most probably refer to Peada, son of King Penda of the Mercians, who is mentioned by Bede as king of the Middle Angles (*Hist. Eccl.* bk. III, ch. 21). This dates the coins within the period 655–7. The suggestion that the runes refer to Penda himself (who died in 655) is, I feel, less plausible, despite Peada's short and obscure reign.[1]

The use of the *a*-rune for *êa* suggests that, as in the case of the Scanomodu coin, a separate *êa*-rune was not yet in general use. The *p*-rune corresponds to that of the Thames fuþorc, whereas the *d*-rune still retains, as on the Scanomodu coin, its traditional Germanic form.

Another set of Mercian coins, also here illustrated, shows the name ᚫᚦᛁᛚ(ᛁ)ᚱᚫᛞ *æþil(i)ræd*, that is Æthelred, king of Mercia, 675–704. The *d*-rune is the same as above.

East Anglian coins. British Museum. Figs. 15 and 16.

As examples of typical mixed Latin–runic inscriptions, such as were increasingly common from the beginning of the eighth century, the following may be cited:

BEOᚾᚾᚪ REX *Beonna Rex*, probably referring to Beorna, king of East Anglia, dated by Florence of Worcester A.D. 758.

EðILᛒERᚻT: ᛚᚢᛚ *Eðelberht: Lul*, probably the names of Æthelberht, who died 794, and of a moneyer Lul.

Bibliography

KEARY, C. F. *A Catalogue of English Coins in the British Museum.* Anglo-Saxon Series, vol. I, edited by R. S. Poole (London, 1887).

HILL, G. F. *A Guide to the Department of Coins and Medals in the British Museum* (London, 1922).

[1] H. M. Chadwick, *Studies in Anglo-Saxon Institutions* (Cambridge, 1905), p. 3, n. 4. Thus also Bruce Dickins (orally).

2. WEAPONS

The Thames scramasax. British Museum. Fig. 7.

Found in the River Thames in London in 1857, the scramasax consists of a single-sided blade and a long point. Its present length is 2 ft. 4½ in. The runes and ornamentation are inlaid with brass and silver wire. The inscription consists of the complete twenty-eight-letter fuþorc (see Table IV) and the word ᛒᛠᚷᚾᚩᚦ *bêagnoþ*, the name probably of the maker or first owner. The runes have been discussed in chapter IV.

The provenance of this find suggests ultimately Southern, presumably Kentish, origin, and this is borne out by the fact that only the twenty-eight runes of the first Anglo-Saxon extension of the older fuþark are represented at a time when the final additional runes must already have been in use in the North of England.

Any attempt to date the scramasax must inevitably take account of the fact that this type of weapon belongs to a period when Danish or Viking influence was making itself felt in this country. It is therefore best assigned to the ninth century.

The Chessel Down sword. British Museum. Fig. 10.

This sword was found last century in a pagan Jutish cemetery at Chessel Down, Isle of Wight. Made of iron, its present overall length is 3 ft. 1 in. The runes are inscribed on the inner side of the silver scabbard-mount, and read ᚫᚳᚩ: ᛋᚩᚱᛁ *æco: sœri*. Stephens' interpretation, of which the gist is 'woe to the weapons (of the foe)', is valueless, although he read the runes correctly and saw that the division marks suggest that the inscription consists of two words. G. Hempl mistakenly, I believe, regards the fourth rune as an incompletely closed ᚹ *w*, reading *æco wœri* which he renders 'self-defence', 'than which there could hardly be a more appropriate legend for a sword'.

No doubt Hempl was right in suggesting that the runes spell the weapon's name, but it seems to me more likely that the name implies attack rather than defence, as in the case, for example, of the Øvre Stabu and Kowel spearheads. I therefore prefer to regard *æco* as a variant of the W.S. noun *ēaca*, 'increase',[1] and *sœri* as a Kentish form of the dative–instrumental of O.E. *sorg*, 'sorrow, pain', rendering 'increase to pain'.[2] The vocalisation of *g* in *sœrgi* becoming *sœri* is a typical early Kenticism; *œ* for *o* occurs in the corresponding verbal form *sœr(g)endi* in the mixed Mercian–Kentish Épinal glossary of about A.D. 700; and the dative–instrumental ending *-i* is found, for example, in *cæstri* (Franks casket) and *rodi* (Ruthwell).[3]

Such an interpretation is necessarily tentative, but the naming of weapons in this manner, to enhance their power to inflict wounds, follows common runic tradition. The forms of the words as well as the transitional shape of the *c*-rune (between < and normal Anglo-Saxon ᚳ, as on the Scanomodu coin) suggest a date somewhere in the seventh or early eighth century. The shape of the *s*-rune, which Hempl deemed so late as to be incompatible with the archaic *c*-rune, is only a variant form, not necessarily late, corresponding to the ᚴ of St Cuthbert's shrine (Durham) of A.D. 698. This shape probably represents at first simply an upward extension of the third (the lower right) stroke of ᛋ, as in the form ᛋ of Bewcastle, and then a formal simplification into ᛆ, or facing the other way ᚴ. To assign such a form invariably to a late date is to overlook the extent to which variant and transitional shapes of runes could and did exist side by side in Anglo-Saxon no less than in Germanic usage.

That the inscription is of Kentish (Jutish) origin is suggested by the form of the words as well as by the place where the weapon was found.

Bibliography

HEMPL, G. 'The runic inscription on the Isle of Wight sword.' *Publ. Mod. Lang. Assoc. America*, vol. 18; n.s. vol. 11, pp. 95 ff. 1903.

[1] Comparable forms occur in the Épinal and Corpus glossaries, as well as in later Kentish sources.

[2] Or 'augmenter of pain'. Mrs H. R. Davidson, F.S.A., has kindly drawn my attention to similar O.N. sword-names like *Angrvaðill* and *Kvǫl*.

[3] As both these are, like *sorg*, feminine *ō*-stem nouns the *-i* ending may be regarded as analogical. Cf. Sievers–Brunner, *Altenglische Grammatik* (1942), para. 252, n. 1. A different point of view is that of Professor C. L. Wrenn who suggests (*Trans. Philol. Soc.* (1943), pp. 19 ff.) that this and other forms on the Ruthwell Cross are deliberate (but faulty) archaisms.

3. SEPULCHRAL STONES

The Sandwich stone. Royal Museum, Canterbury. Figs. 26, 27.

Two stones of roughly the same dimensions were found about 1830 near Sandwich, Kent. Both have inscribed panels, but only on one is the inscription now legible. This latter stone measures 1 ft. 4 in. in height, 6 sq. in. at the base and 4 sq. in. at the top.

The runes read ᚱᚫᚢᚠᛒᚢᛚ *ræhæbul*, most probably a personal name. The rough nature of the stone, the absence of any Christian marks or ornamentation, as well as the archaic nature of the name, preserving intervocalic *h*, speak for an early date, certainly before the middle of the seventh century. Equally archaic is the form of the *h*-rune (cf. Vadstena), which in normal Anglo-Saxon usage has the form ᚺ.

It is therefore quite possible that we have here the only likely English example of a heathen sepulchral stone, probably originally intended for the inside of a grave. Its size and shape speak against its having been used or intended as a 'pillow-stone' like those of Hartlepool (see below), and it is possible that the name Ræhæbul was that of the rune-master rather than of the deceased. That the inscription originated where it was found, in Kent, may be legitimately assumed.

Another probably heathen runic stone was actually found inside a tumulus at 'Pippin Castle' (near Harrogate, Yorks) in 1901, but its inscription *suna* is in Scandinavian runes and probably no earlier than the tenth century.

The Hartlepool stones. St Hilda's Church, Hartlepool, and Black Gate Museum, Newcastle upon Tyne. Fig. 30.

Several small sepulchral slabs were found in 1833 on the site of an early Northumbrian monastic cemetery at Hartlepool, Co. Durham. As some of these were discovered under the skulls in the graves they are sometimes known as 'pillow-stones' or, more generally, as 'name-stones'. Similar stones have been found at Lindisfarne, another ancient Northumbrian monastic site. The cross design marks the stones as Christian although the use of pillow-stones dates back to Anglo-Saxon heathendom. Some of the stones bear inscriptions in insular lettering; of two stones with runic inscriptions one, stone no. 2, is illustrated in Fig. 30.

The latter stone measures 8¾ in. by 6¼ in. by 2⅞ in. The runes are ᚻᛁᛚᛞᛞᛁᚷᚣᚦ *hilddigyþ*, a female personal name, more properly *hildigyþ*; the *d*-rune appears duplicated in error, while the *g*-rune is added above the word between *i* and *y*.

The other runic stone, no. 1, measures very nearly 11½ in. square by 4½ in. and bears the symbols for 'Alpha' and 'Omega' followed beneath by the runes ᚻᛁᛚᛞᛁᚦᚱᚣᚦ *hildiþryþ*, again a female personal name.

The names are presumably those of nuns buried in the respective graves. The monastery was originally founded about A.D. 640; by 686 it had become a nunnery. As it was sacked by the Danes around 800 the stones most probably belong to the eighth century. This dating also conforms with the retention of final *-i* in *hildi-*, later Old English *-e* as in Hildeburh, the name of Finn's queen (*Beowulf*, 1071, 1114).

Of the two forms of the *d*-rune, ᛞ and ⋈, the first is the more common in Anglo-Saxon usage; the second is the more archaic and occurs in several early inscriptions, such as the Scanomodu and Pada coins. Characteristic of normal Anglo-Saxon usage are the shapes of the *h* and *y* runes.

The Dover stone. Dover Corporation Museum. Fig. 31.

This Kentish stone, found at Dover early last century, is, unlike the Sandwich stone, unmistakably Christian. It is also of much later date. A proper sepulchral slab, it measures 6 ft. 2 in. in length, 2 ft. 3 in. in width at the place where the runes occur; and the average thickness is about 7 in. The runes are preceded by a cross and read ✱ᛁᛋᛚᚻᛠᚱᛞ *jislhêard*, probably the personal name of the deceased, Gislheard.

The first rune, *j*, is probably best explained as a formal variant of the types †, ᛄ, Φ, found elsewhere in Anglo-Saxon usage, although it will be recalled that the form ✱ is not unknown in common Germanic usage (e.g. the Noleby stone, Fig. 28). It occurs with the same phonetic value [j] in the name *jilsuiþ* on the third Thornhill cross fragment (see below) and in the name *adugislu* on the yew weaving-slay of Westeremden (Friesland; Fig. 23) which belongs to the eighth or early ninth century. The second rune, here transcribed *i*, must denote a vowel, presumably the high front vowel between *e* and *i* generally denoted by this rune already in common Germanic usage; it occurs with the same value on the Brunswick whalebone casket, a Northumbrian piece of the early eighth century. The shape of the *ſ*-rune lies half-way between the common Anglo-Saxon ч and the simplified Υ of Thames, Chessel Down, and St Cuthbert's shrine at Durham; its closest parallel is on the Bewcastle cross-shaft, although this is of much earlier date. Apart from the distinctly archaic *ſ*-rune on the Scanomodu coin, all these forms of the *ſ*-rune were probably current simultaneously and I do not believe that any chronological significance should be attached to them.

As there are no early features either in the runes or in the name itself, and as this is obviously a Christian monument, the date of the inscription is probably no earlier than the ninth century; it may even belong to the early part of the tenth.

Bibliography

BROWN, G. B. 'The Hartlepool Tombstones.' *Proc. Soc. Antiq. Scotland*, vol. 53, pp. 195 ff. 1919; and *The Arts in Early England*, vol. 5, pp. 58 ff. London, 1921.

DICKINS, B. 'The Sandwich Runic Inscription RÆHÆBUL.' *Festschrift für Gustav Neckel*, ed. by K. H. Schlottig, pp. 83 ff. Leipzig, 1938.

SCOTT, F. S. 'The Hildithryth Stone and the Other Hartlepool Name-Stones.' *Archæologia Aeliana*, vol. 34, pp. 196 ff. 1956.

4. CROSS FRAGMENTS

The Hackness cross fragments. Hackness Church. Fig. 33.

Two fragments of a limestone cross-shaft stand in the south aisle of the parish church at Hackness, near Scarborough, Yorks. The two pieces probably represent the original lower and upper portions of the shaft; the centre piece of approximately 5½ ft. in length is missing. The various panels that remain on the four sides of the shaft show a number of inscriptions, some foliage and interlaced pattern carvings, and the head of a figure of Christ on the west face.

The inscriptions consist of the following: (i) three Latin inscriptions in Roman characters; (ii) an inscription on the lower south panel in a pseudo-Ogham script; and (iii) two lines of runes, followed by three and a half lines of *hahalruna*[1] and the Latin word *ora* on the present centre panel on the east face.

The stone, and consequently the carving and inscriptions, have suffered badly from weathering and careless handling so that much is now defaced beyond hope of recognition. The Latin inscriptions, however, have been sufficiently deciphered to yield the indication that the cross was erected to commemorate the abbess Oedilburga and perhaps other members of the religious community of Hackness, the Hacanos of Bede, founded as a cell of Whitby in 680 for a community of nuns.

The pseudo-Ogham inscription on the south face has never been deciphered; it is too short and now too mutilated to make a reading or interpretation possible. The suggestion has been made that it represents a kind of secret code known only to the inmates of the community, based on proper Ogham script which it resembles in appearance and probably in principle. That, however, is as far as any explanation can hope to go.

Unfortunately, much the same verdict applies also to the two runic inscriptions on the east face. The present position of the fragments, within less than 3 ft. of the east wall of the church, makes the runes extremely difficult to examine, and our photograph had to be taken with the help of a mirror and very careful lighting in order to bring out what is still visible of the runes. What can be deciphered appears to be this:

$$+ \text{M M h (?R) I . P R} \qquad + m\ m\ c\ (?r)\ i\ .\ w\ \alpha$$
$$\text{R + . * h R F X} \qquad \alpha\ n\ .\ j\ c\ \alpha\ \alpha g$$

Others have offered different readings, but none of them, as they stand, make any sense whatever, and we are again compelled to

---

[1] See below. The name *hahalruna* has recently been explained by reference to O.H.G. *hahal*, 'a pothanger with a rack', an instrument whose appearance is not unlike the *hahalruna*. See Derolez, *op. cit.* p. 133.

assume that some kind of secret code is employed, perhaps a mere substitution or transposition of letters, possibly intended as a clue to the *hahalruna* following below. The suggestion that these two lines contain 'a list of names or other words written straightforwardly but abbreviated so as to be unintelligible to those to whom the names are unknown'[1] seems to us unlikely. But the inscription is too short to afford sufficient material for solving the cipher; another age-old runic mystery defies us.

There follow three and a half lines of *hahalruna*,[2] again too defaced to allow a clear reading. The principle of this form of runic cryptography is quite simple: the fuþorc would be divided into several groups; the lateral strokes on the left of the vertical indicate the group intended, and those on the right indicate the number of the rune required within that particular group. Thus if, for example, the common Germanic fuþark is divided into its three *ættir* of eight runes each, then ↑ would signify the first rune in the first group of eight, i.e. *f*; ↑ group I, rune 2, i.e. *u*; ⍦ group III, rune 4, i.e. *m*; etc. In the present instance, however, assuming the same principle to have been employed, the fuþorc appears to have been divided into four sections, as some of the *hahalruna* have four laterals on the left. The greatest number of laterals on the right is eight.[3] As far as can be judged the inscription consisted originally of thirty-five *hahalruna*, three lines of ten each and five runes in the fourth line followed by *ora*, 'pray', in Roman capitals.

This system of *hahalruna* cryptography is by no means unique to the Hackness cross. Similar inscriptions have been discovered, for example, at Maeshowe (Orkney) and at several places in Scandinavia. In this connection the Swedish Rök stone, 'a regular catalogue of cryptic systems', deserves special mention. In addition we possess a number of continental MSS. of the ninth to eleventh century containing the so-called *Isruna Tract* in which several types of runic cryptography,

[1] G. B. Brown, *The Arts in Early England*, vol. 6, pt. 1 (1930), p. 68.
[2] The Hackness runes are sometimes referred to as 'twig-runes' or 'tree-runes', but in the latter, the Icelandic *kvistrúnar*, the 'branches' go upwards.
[3] Recognisably so on our photograph in the case of the first and the last of the *hahalruna*.

including *hahalruna*, are explained and illustrated.[1] What makes
the Hackness inscription so interesting, however, is that it
employs four different types of script of which only the Latin is
straightforward, and it is all the more tantalising that of the
three cryptic inscriptions, the pseudo-Ogham, the runic, and
the *hahalruna*, none is sufficiently long or well preserved to
make a correct reading or interpretation possible.[2] All that can
safely be said is that the inscriptions belong to Northumbria and
are probably of the early eighth century.

The Lancaster cross fragment. British Museum. Fig. 34.

This stone cross fragment was found in 1807 at St Mary's
churchyard, Lancaster, and is now in the British Museum. Its
present height is 3 ft., the original breadth across the arms being
1 ft. 9 in. A runic inscription of three lines is set in a panel
on the front of the shaft just below the cross-head. It reads:

ᚷᛁᛒᛁᛞᚫᚦᚠᚩ	gibidæþfo
ᚱᚫᚳᚢᛁᛒᚪᛏ	ræcynibal
ᚦᚳᚢᚦᛒᛖᚱᛖ	þcuþbere

that is: 'gibidæþ foræ cynibalþ cuþbere-', 'pray for Cynibalth
Cuthber...'; the end of the third line can no longer be
deciphered; there is room for possibly two more runes.
Stephens suggested completing *cuþbærehting*, 'Cuthbertson', for
which, at least without some ligature, there does not seem to be
enough space; we can, however, at least safely complete the
name Cuthbert by assuming *-ct* or *-ht* and regard these two
names as those of separate persons for both of whom prayer is
requested. The formula is a common one on Anglo-Saxon
crosses and gravestones both in Latin and runic inscriptions.
Among runic parallels are, for example, the biliteral Falstone
stone, the Urswick (Furness) cross fragment, and the Overchurch (Wirral) stone.

The language of the inscription points to early eighth-century
Northumbria; typical of the Northumbrian dialect is the

---

[1] Cf. Derolez, *op. cit.* ch. II.
[2] Derolez's tentative transliteration of the *hahalruna* (*op. cit.* p. 142, n. 1)
contributes little towards their interpretation.

intrusive ('svarabhakti') vowel in the final syllable of *cuþbere-*, comparable to *wylif*, *-berig* (Franks casket), *-burug* (Bewcastle), *worohtæ* (Kirkheaton, Yorks, stone), etc.[1]

The runes are straightforward; *-dd-* is simplified to *-d-* in *gibidæþ* according to common runic practice.[2] All the runes belong to the common Anglo-Saxon twenty-eight-letter fuþorc.

The Thornhill fragments. Church of St Michael, Thornhill. Figs. 35–7.

In 1875–6 and 1881 respectively there came to light in the Church of St Michael, Thornhill, near Dewsbury, Yorkshire, several fragments of carved sandstone crosses of which three bear runic inscriptions.

The first (Thornhill *A*, fig. 35, runes traced) reads:

+ ᛖᚦᛖᛚᛒᛖ	+ eþelbe
ᚱᚻᛏ: ᛋᛖᛏᛏᚫᚠᛏᛖ	rht: settæfte
ᚱ: ᛖᚦᛖᛚᚹᛁᚾᛁ:	r: eþelwini:...

that is: 'eþelberht settæ (æ)fter eþelwini...', 'Ethelberht set (up this cross) after Ethelwini...'. Stephens read several further runes ᛞᛖᚱᛁᛝ *deriŋ* in the lower right-hand margin, that is: *dering*(æ), 'Dering', perhaps 'son of Deor(a)'. Vietor suggested a possible *l* or *æ* in the margin; something may well have been added here, but cannot now be deciphered. Collingwood conjectured that the inscription concluded with the customary formula 'pray for him'.

The second fragment (Thornhill *B*, fig. 36, runes traced) reads:

+ ᛠᛞᚱᛖᛞ	+ êadred
ᛋᛖᛏᛖᚫᚠᛏᛖ	seteæfte
ᛠᛏᛖᛁᚾᚾᛖ	êateinne

that is: 'eadred sete æfte(r) eateinne', 'Eadred set (up this cross) after Eata'. This and the previous inscription both employ a

[1] Sievers–Brunner, *Altenglische Grammatik* (Halle, 1942), para. 164.

[2] This word is discussed by A. S. C. Ross in *Mod. Lang. Notes*, vol. 47 (1932), p. 377.

common formula although the spelling varies. The traditional runic practice of writing successive identical sounds once only persists in the shared *æ* of *settæfter* (*A*) and in the single *t* of *sete* (*B*), whereas normal scribal practice rules in the duplicated *t* of the former word, and in the presence of both the final vowel of *sete* and the following initial *æ*.

In *A* the form of the *h*-rune is like that of the Dover stone a slight modification of the Anglo-Saxon norm, probably without any particular significance. The final ligature read by Stephens is very indistinct and by now largely conjectural, so that the end of the last line must remain doubtful, unless Stephens' reading is followed.

B is straightforward except for the last line where the use of ᛇ presents a real difficulty. In Old English, it will be remembered, this rune denotes either a high front vowel as on the Brunswick casket or the Dover stone, or else the spirant [ç] as on the Ruthwell Cross. Neither fits in here; if the name intended was *Eata*, then the correct form here would be *Eatan*. A possible solution would be to assume that the name intended was *Eatinge*, 'son of Eata'. In that case the second *n* is either simply an error for *g*, or else the rune ᛡ was originally carved here with the value *g* as on the Brunswick casket but is now no longer visible as such; this, however, presupposes that the carver used the two runes *n* and *g* instead of the normal ᛝ [ŋ] = *ng*. The insertion of ᛖ *e* after the *t*-rune could be a mechanical error prompted by the sequence ᛏᛖ *te* in the line immediately above. Errors of omission and of faulty addition are not unknown in runic inscriptions; the second Hartlepool stone (cf. above) furnishes a likely example. Bruce Dickins suggests that the name, which he transcribes *êatezʒnne*, stands for Eadþegne.

The longest of the inscriptions (Thornhill *C*, fig. 37) consists of three and a half lines and reads:

+ ᛡᛁᛚᛋᚢᛁᚦ: ᚪᚱᚫᚱᛞᛖ: ᚫᚠᛏᛖ	+ jilsuiþ: arærde: æfte
ᛒᛖᚱᚻᛏᛋᚢᛁᚦᛖ. ᛒᛖᚳᚢᚾ	berhtsuiþe. bekun
ᚩᚾᛒᛖᚱᚷᛁᚷᛖᛒᛁᛞᛞᚪᚦ	onbergigebiddaþ
ᚦᚫᚱ: ᛋᚪᚢᛚᛖ	þær: saule

that is: 'jilsuiþ aræede æfte(r) berhtsuiþe bekun on bergi; gebiddaþ þær saule', 'Gilsuith raised up this beacon after Berhtsuith on her tomb; pray for her soul'. The beacon can only be the monument, i.e. the cross, itself, apparently erected by one nun in memory of another. More details can hardly be deduced from these few words.[1] Stephens and others have read *at* as the first word in line 3, but I think Bruce Dickins is right in seeing *on* there, with all due reservations.

The language of the three inscriptions points to Northumbria at the end of the eighth century or in the first half of the ninth. The only distinctively Northumbrian rune is ⋏ k^1, used before a back vowel in *bekun* as on the Ruthwell Cross (*kwomu*); it probably came into use in the course of the eighth century. The first rune in *C* has the same sound-value as on the Dover stone. The ligature ⋈ *dd* represents an obvious graphical economy, though it departs from the earlier convention not to write double sounds. The uncertainty displayed by the three Thornhill inscriptions with regard to double sounds suggests that the older runic practice was giving way before the more normal manuscript usage. The short *i*-rune in the first line of *C* appears to have been first omitted in error and then inserted as far as possible; all the other *i*-runes are quite regular.

Bibliography

KEMBLE, J. M. 'Further notes on the runic cross at Lancaster.' *Archaeologia*, vol. 29, pp. 76 ff. 1842.

COLLINGWOOD, W. G. 'Anglian and Anglo-Danish sculpture in the East Riding of Yorkshire.' *Yorks. Archaeol. Journal*, vol. 21, pp. 278 ff. 1911. (Hackness.)

—— 'Anglian and Anglo-Danish sculpture in the West Riding of Yorkshire....' *Yorks. Archaeol. Journal*, vol. 23, pp. 243 ff. 1915. (Thornhill.)

BROWN, G. B. *The Arts in Early England*, vol. 6, pt. 1, ch. III. 1930. (Hackness.)

---

[1] Whitbread, 'The Thornhill Cross Inscription', *Notes and Queries*, vol. 193, (1948), p. 156, suggests that this inscription, if divided between *berhtsuiþe* and *bekun*, falls 'into two lines of loosely alliterative Old English verse'. For this he follows Collingwood's reading of the first name as *Igilsuiþ*, but metrically the lines are highly dubious in any case.

WHITBREAD, L. 'The Thornhill Cross Inscription.' *Notes and Queries*, vol. 193, p. 156. 1948.

DEROLEZ, R. *Runica Manuscripta. The English Tradition*, pp. 140 ff. 1954. (Hackness.)

5. THE RUTHWELL CROSS

Ruthwell Church, Dumfriesshire. Figs. 38–40.

This 18 ft. tall stone cross, a splendid specimen of early eighth-century Northumbrian art, is undoubtedly the best known and most imposing of all the remaining English runic stone monuments; its closest parallel is the artistically similar and probably contemporary shaft of the runic cross at Bewcastle (Cumberland; Fig. 41).

The Ruthwell Cross was removed from its place in the parish church and broken into several pieces as a result of an Act of Assembly of the Scottish Church in 1642 directed against 'idolatrous monuments'. In 1802 the remains were gathered and the cross set up in the grounds of the manse with an additional transom, the original transom having been lost. In 1887, to avoid further damage from the weather, the cross was returned into the church where it now stands.

In addition to lavish sculpture ornamentation, the cross bears inscriptions in Roman and runic characters. The former refer to the ten main sculptured panels which represent Christian figures and biblical scenes as follows:

On the north side: (1) John the Baptist bearing the Agnus Dei; (2) Christ standing on two animals; (3) the saints Paulus and Antonius breaking a loaf of bread; (4) the flight into Egypt; (5) Indistinct remains of a figure subject, possibly the Nativity.

On the south side: (1) the Visitation; (2) Christ and Mary Magdalene; (3) Christ healing the blind man; (4) the Annunciation; (5) the Crucifixion.

The main runic inscription is carved on the two narrower sides of the cross, east and west, above and along the side margins of the long panels containing foliage and animal sculpture; some isolated runic words occurring elsewhere will be discussed separately below. The principal inscription is devoted entirely to certain passages, in the Northumbrian dialect of the early eighth century, of the beautiful Old English poem *The Dream of the Rood* in which the Cross itself speaks of the agony and glory of the Crucifixion. For convenience the runes are here given in separate words and in lines corresponding to those of the full text of the poem in the Vercelli Codex. No marks of division are used on the cross. Some likely readings are added in brackets, and points are used to indicate the probable number of missing runes.[1]

On the east side (north-east):

Line 39 ..ᚷᛖᚱᛖᛞᚫ ᚻᛁᚾᚫ ᚸᚩᛞ ᚪᛚᛗᛖᛇᛏᛏᛁᚷ
geredæ hinæ g̅od almeȝttig

40 ᚦᚪ ᚻᛖ ᚹᚪᛚᛞᛖ ᚩᚾ ᚸᚪᛚᚸᚢ ᚷᛁᛋᛏᛁᚸᚪ
þa he walde on g̅alg̅u gistig̅a

41 .ᚩᛞᛁᚷ ᚠ... ....ᛗᛖᚾ
(m)odig f[ ] men

42 .ᚢᚸ. [about thirty characters lost]
(b)ug̅(a)

On the east side (south-east):

Line 44 ....ᛁᚳ ᚱᛁᛁᚳᚾᚫ ᛤᚣᚾᛁᛝᚳ
ic riicnæ k̅yniŋc

45 ᚻᛠᚠᚢᚾᚫᛋ ᚻᛚᚪᚠᚪᚱᛞ ᚻᚫᛚᛞᚪ ᛁᚳ ᚾᛁ ᛞᚩᚱᛋᛏᚫ
hêafunæs hlafard hælda ic ni dorstæ

48 ᛒᛁᛋᛗᚫᚱᚫᛞᚢ ᚢᛝᛤᛖᛏ ᛗᛖᚾ ᛒᚪ ᚫᛏᚸᚪᛞ..ᛁᚳ...
bismærædu uŋk̅et men ba ætg̅ad(ræ) ic (wæs)
ᛗᛁᚦ ᛒᛚᚩᛞᚫ .ᛁᛋᛏᛖᛗᛁ.
miþ blodæ (b)istemi(d)

49 ᛒᛁ [about forty characters lost]
bi

On the west side (south-west):

Line 56 ᛣᚱᛁᛋᛏ ᚹᚫᛋ ᚩᚾ ᚱᚩᛞᛁ
krist wæs on rodi

[1] The method of transcription follows that of Bruce Dickins, *Leeds Studies in English* (1932), pp. 17f. and Dickins and Ross, *The Dream of the Rood* (4th ed. London, 1954).

Line 57 ᚾᛈᛖᚦᚱᚪ ᚦᛗᚱ ᚠᚾᛄᚠ ᚠᛦᚱᚱᛗᛉ ᛚᛈᛖᛄᚾ

hweþræ þer fusæ fêarran kwomu .

58 ᚠᚦᚦᛁᚾᚠ ᛏᛁᛏ ᛗᛄᚾᛈᛗ ᛁᚻ ᚦᛗᛏ ᛗᛏ ᛒᛁᚻ...

æþþilæ til anum ic þæt al bih(êald)

59 ᛋ... ᛁᚻ ᚠᚠᚻ ᛗᛁ. ᛋᛖᚱᚷᚾᛈᛗ ᚷᛁᛈᚱᛖ..ᛈ

s(aræ) ic wæs mi(þ) sorḡum gidrœ(fi)d

ᚾ.ᛉᛉ [about eighteen characters lost]

h(n)aḡ

On the west side (north-west):

Line 62 ᛗᛁᚦ ᛋᛏᚱᛗᛏᚾᛈᛗ ᚷᛁᛈᚾᛋᚻᛈᛗᛈ

miþ strelum giwundad

63 ᛗᛏᛗᚷᛈᛈᚾᛉ ᚻᛁᚠ ᚻᛁᚻᚠ ᛏᛁᛗᛈᛖᚱᛁᚷᚾᛉ ᚷᛁᛋᛏᛈᛈᛈᚾᛉ

alegdun hiæ hinæ limwœrignæ gistoddun

ᚻᛁᛗ.....ᛏᛁᚻᚠᛋ ..ᚠ..ᛈ

him.....licæs (hêa)f(du)m

64 ..ᚾᛉ.ᛈᛈᚾ. ᚻᛁ.ᚦᛗ [about twenty characters lost]

(bi)hêa(l)du(n) hi(æ) þe(r)

For the sake of comparison the relevant passage of the Vercelli text of the poem is here quoted with translation, the lines paralleled on the cross being printed in italics:

Ongyrede hine þa geong hæleð (þæt wæs god ælmihtig)   39
strang ond stiðmod. Gestah he on gealgan heanne,
modig on manigra gesyhðe, þa he wolde mancyn lysan.
Bifode ic þa me se beorn ymbclypte. Ne dorste ic hwæðre bugan to eorðan,
feallan to foldan sceatum, ac ic sceolde fæste standan.
Rod wæs ic aræred. Ahof ic ricne cyning,
heofona hlaford, hyldan me ne dorste.   45
Þurhdrifan hi me mid deorcan næglum. On me syndon þa dolg gesiene,
opene inwidhlemmas. Ne dorste ic hira nænigum sceððan.
Bysmeredon hie unc butu ætgædere. Eall ic wæs mid blode bestemed,
begoten of þæs guman sidan, siððan he hæfde his gast onsended.
Feala ic on þam beorge gebiden hæbbe   50
wraðra wyrda. Geseah ic weruda god
þearle þenian. Þystro hæfdon
bewrigen mid wolcnum wealdendes hræw,
scirne sciman, sceadu forðeode,
wann under wolcnum. Weop eal gesceaft,   55

cwiðdon cyninges fyll. Crist wæs on rode.
   Hwæðere þær fuse feorran cwoman
to þam æðelinge. Ic þæt eall beheold.
Sare ic wæs mid sorgum gedrefed, hnag ic hwæðre þam secgum to handa,
eaðmod elne mycle. Genamon hie þær ælmihtigne god,   60
ahofon hine of ðam hefian wite. Forleton me þa hilderincas
standan steame bedrifenne; eall ic wæs mid strælum forwundod.
Aledon hie ðær limwerigne, gestodon him æt his lices heafdum,
beheoldon hie ðær heofenes dryhten, ond he hine ðær hwile reste,
meðe æfter ðam miclan gewinne.   65

Then the young Warrior, God, the All-Wielder,
Put off His raiment, steadfast and strong;
With lordly mood in the sight of many
He mounted the Cross to redeem mankind.
When the Hero clasped me I trembled in terror,
But I dared not bow me nor bend to earth;
I must needs stand fast. Upraised as the Rood
I held the High King, the Lord of heaven.
I dared not bow! With black nails driven
Those sinners pierced me; the prints are clear,
The open wounds. I dared injure none.
They mocked us both. I was wet with blood
From the Hero's side when He sent forth his spirit.
   Many a bale I bore on that hill-side
Seeing the Lord in agony outstretched.
Black darkness covered with clouds God's body,
That radiant splendour. Shadow went forth
Wan under heaven; all creation wept
Bewailing the King's death. Christ was on the Cross.
   Then many came quickly, faring from far,
Hurrying to the Prince. I beheld it all.
Sorely smitten with sorrow in meekness I bowed
To the hands of men. From his heavy and bitter pain
They lifted Almighty God. Those warriors left me
Standing bespattered with blood; I was wounded with spears.
Limb-weary they laid Him down; they stood at his head,
Looked on the Lord of heaven as He lay there at rest
From his bitter ordeal all forspent.[1]

   The precise relationship between the poem and the Ruthwell
runic inscription and the inscription of the so-called Brussels

---

[1] Translated by C. W. Kennedy, *Early English Christian Poetry* (London, 1952).

Cross[1] remains conjectural. The most likely hypothesis is that the runic passages represent the main portion of an original Northumbrian poem which was later expanded into the much longer poem preserved in the Vercelli Codex. On the cross the function of the runes is largely ornamental: they enhance the fervent Christian piety that is revealed in the monument itself and the motifs of its sculptural decoration.

The smaller runic inscriptions on the cross are independent of *The Dream of the Rood*, and their interpretation is so dubious as hardly to warrant the attempt. In the sinister margin of the upper panel on the east face there appear the runes ᛞᚫᚷᛁᛋᚷᚫᚠ *dægisgæf*, which may be a personal name. The attempt to relate it to the poem by reading '(wœpi)dæ gisgæf(t)', corresponding to the Vercelli 'weop eal gesceaft', 'all creation wept' (line 55), fails to account satisfactorily for its isolated appearance on this upper panel, divorced both in space and in the method of inscribing from the rest of the text.

An even more disputed inscription is that on the south face of the cross-head itself—originally the north side—which reads ᛗᚫᚠᚪᚢᚩᚦ *mæfauœþo*. This has defied all satisfactory interpretation. Stephens quite unjustifiably read *Cadmon* on the cross as well, rendering the whole as 'Cadmon me fawed (made)', thereby adding weight to the wholly unfounded and unacceptable theory that *The Dream of the Rood* is to be ascribed to the Anglo-Saxon poet Cædmon whose story Bede tells in *Hist. Eccl.* bk. IV, ch. 24.

The remaining runes occur in the margins of the Visitation panel on the south face and appear to have formed part of the explanatory inscription; this is exceptional because elsewhere on the cross these marginal inscriptions are in Latin characters. The runes read ᛗ....ᛗ..ᛁ...ᚱ *m m i r* and ᛞᚩᛗᛁᚾᚾᚫ *dominnæ* respectively; the first group is really too fragmentary to permit an interpretation, the second renders a Latin word in runes as on the back of the Franks casket (see below, p. 101). The Ruthwell Cross runes represent an extension of the common Anglo-Saxon twenty-eight-letter fuþorc, although six

[1] For details of the Brussels Cross see Dickins and Ross, *op. cit.* pp. 13 ff.

runes of the final Northumbrian maximum of thirty-three—
j, p, x, ĩo, q, št—do not occur; the last three were probably not
yet in common use. Both the Ruthwell and Bewcastle crosses
employ various symbols in an attempt to distinguish between
the several phonetic values of Old English *g, c,* and *k.* Bewcastle, however, is less consistent and includes some obvious
errors; thus on the latter monument the initial sound of the
syllable *kin-* appears correctly as ᛢ in *k̄yniŋ* on the main panel,
but wrongly as ᚳ in *kyniburug* (north face). Ruthwell is more
consistent: before front vowels it uses ᛢ *k*[II] (transliterated with
the help of a line above the letter) in *uŋk̄et, k̄yniŋc;* ᚳ *k*[I] is used
before a consonant in *krist,* before back vowels in *kwomu;* and
ᚻ *c* occurs in *ic, riicnæ, k̄yniŋc,* and *licæs.* Of these runes ᛢ is
confined to Ruthwell and Bewcastle; it probably represents a
formal variant of ᚷ *g*[II] (also transliterated with a line above), the
velar sound [ɤ] used in *ḡod, ḡalḡu,* which also figures in the
thirty-three-letter fuþorc of Cotton MS. Otho B x. The *gifu-*
rune, ᚷ *g,* is quite normally employed in *geredæ, alegdun,* etc.
On Bewcastle (west face) it is used also for the initial sound of
gessus, 'Jesus', a usage paralleled by the form *giuþeasu,* 'Jews', on
the back of the Franks casket.

The rune ᛋ occurs only once on the Ruthwell Cross, as the
fifth letter in the word *almeʒttig,* 'almighty' (line 39, N.E. face),
where it clearly stands for the spirant [ç], pronounced with the
following dental as in German *nicht.* The doubling of the
t-rune in this word, as of *þ* in *æþþilæ, d* in *gistoddun,* and *n* in
dominnæ does not imply that double consonants were actually
pronounced; most probably the common runic rule of writing
single consonants for double here operates *vice versa.* Bewcastle has double consonants in *setton,* 'they set up', as well as in
.essus and *gessus,* 'Jesus', and *Kristtus,* 'Christ'. Bewcastle also
has several ligatures, including three times ᚦᚢ *þu,* whereas
Ruthwell has only one, ᛗᚫ *mæ,* on the cross-head.

The date of both crosses has been considerably debated on
artistic, linguistic, and runological grounds. In the case of
Bewcastle the likeliest view still is that the cross was erected in
memory of Alcfrith (*fl.* 664), the son of Oswiu, king of

Northumbria, both whose names are mentioned in the main runic panel, and that it records also the name of Alcfrith's wife Cyniburug, daughter of King Penda of the Mercians. The art and epigraphy of both monuments are very similar and are assigned by most recent authorities to the period 670–750. On linguistic and runological grounds the first half of the eighth century is the more acceptable; before this time the additional rune ᛇ was probably not yet in use, while at a later date one should have expected at least the *st*-rune to occur which by the end of the eighth century had found its way across to Friesland to figure three times in the yew wand of Westeremden (Fig. 22).

Bibliography

COOK, A. S. 'The Date of the Ruthwell and Bewcastle Crosses.' *Trans. Connecticut Acad. Arts and Sciences*, vol. 17, pp. 213 ff. 1912.

FORBES, M. D. and DICKINS, B. 'The Inscriptions of the Ruthwell and Bewcastle Crosses and the Bridekirk Font.' *Burlington Magazine*, vol. 25, no. 133, pp. 24 ff. 1914.

HEWISON, J. K. *The Runic Roods of Ruthwell and Bewcastle*. Glasgow, 1914.

BROWNE, G. F. *The Ancient Cross Shafts at Bewcastle and Ruthwell*. Cambridge, 1916.

COLLINGWOOD, W. G. 'The Ruthwell Cross in its relation to other monuments of the Christian age.' *Trans. Dumfriesshire and Galloway Ant. Soc.* pp. 34 ff. 1918.

BROWN, G. B. *The Arts in Early England*, vol. 5, with philological chapters by A. Blyth Webster. London, 1921.

ROSS, A. S. C. 'The Linguistic evidence for the date of the Ruthwell Cross.' *Mod. Lang. Rev.* vol. 28, pp. 145 ff. 1933.

SAXL, F. 'The Ruthwell Cross.' *Journ. Warburg and Courtauld Inst.* vol. 6, pp. 1 ff. 1943.

DICKINS, B. and ROSS, A. S. C. *The Dream of the Rood*. 4th ed., London, 1954. (With further bibliography.)

6. THE FRANKS CASKET

British Museum. Figs. 42–6.

The Franks casket was first discovered in the early years of the nineteenth century in the possession of a French family of Auzon (Haute-Loire), whence the lid and three sides passed to a certain Professor Mathieu of Clermont-Ferrand (Auvergne).

The casket has therefore been variously referred to as either Auzon or Clermont; its most common present designation derives from the name of Sir Augustus Wollaston Franks who acquired the pieces in 1857 and presented them to the British Museum ten years later. The missing (right) side was discovered in 1890 at the Museo Nazionale in Florence and a cast of it has been fitted into its proper place on the remounted casket in the British Museum.

The casket is made of whalebone and measures 9 in. in length, $7\frac{1}{2}$ in. in width, and $5\frac{1}{8}$ in. in height. Of the lid only the central strip remains, and no surrounding inscription survives. The four sides, however, preserve well both their carved panels and their mainly runic and partly Latin inscriptions.

Two similar caskets with Anglo-Saxon runic inscriptions deserve a brief mention here. Both are probably of Northumbrian origin and approximately contemporary with the Franks casket, and also found their way by unknown routes to the Continent. The first is a whalebone casket with animal and tracery ornamentation which in 1815 was acquired by the Herzog Anton Ulrich Museum in Brunswick (Germany). It bears on its base two identical runic inscriptions never satisfactorily interpreted; Bugge and v. Grienberger saw in them a reference to the monastery of Ely, founded in 673; other interpretations, however, have also been attempted.[1] An interesting feature of this inscription is its use of the rune ᚱ for the sound i in hiræ, 'her', and hælig, 'holy', and twice of the symbol ᚹ in lieu of the normal gifu-rune ᚷ.

The second casket is a metal reliquary now in the church of Mortain (Normandy) which has the inscription 'good helpe: æadan þiiosne kiismeel gewarahtæ', 'God help Eada; he made this reliquary'. Two noteworthy features here, apart from the four doubled vowels, are the spelling of æadan with the runes ᚠᚪ æa, an intermediate form, clearly, between the a of the Pada coins and the general subsequent use of ᛠ êa, and the shape of

<hr/>

[1] The Brunswick casket is illustrated in Stephens. Cf. also v. Grienberger, 'Drei Westgermanische Runeninschriften', Z. deut. Philol. vol. 41 (1909), pp. 419ff., and Harder, 'Das Braunschweiger Runenkästchen', Archiv Stud. neueren Sprachen, vol. 162 (1932), pp. 227 ff.

the *d*-rune ᚼ which lies half-way between the common Germanic ᚤ and the normal Old English ᛗ.[1]

In detail the carving and inscriptions of the Franks casket are as follows:

Lid (Fig. 42).

The figure carving depicts a bowman defending a fortified enclosure against an armed band; a stooping female figure sits behind him. Above the bowman are five runes: ᚠᚷᛁᛚᛁ *ægili*, no doubt referring to Egill, brother of Vǫlundr the Smith and master-bowman of Northern legend. The particular incident depicted here is not related in any extant story connected with Egill and we cannot tell who is represented by the horizontal figures above and below the round centre piece (which probably held some sort of handle for lifting the lid or the casket as a whole). The runes present no difficulty or special features.

Front (Fig. 43).

This portion is divided by a narrow band into two panels with unrelated figure subjects. The left shows a scene from Germanic legend: Vǫlundr (Weland) the Smith,[2] standing before the headless body of one of King Niþǫþr's (Nithhad's) sons, is holding a cup made of the victim's skull; in the middle of this panel are shown two female figures, probably the princess Bǫþvildr (Beadohild) and an attendant visiting the smith; while next to them stands a male figure, no doubt Vǫlundr's brother Egill, strangling birds from whose feathers, according to the story, he made wings to effect Vǫlundr's escape from Niþǫþr's captivity.[3]

[1] Cf. M. Cahen and M. Olsen, *L'Inscription runique du coffret de Mortain* (Collection linguistique publ. par la Société de Linguistique de Paris, 32), Paris (1930), and L. Blouet, *Le Chrismale de Mortain*, Bion, par Mortain (1954). Father Blouet suggests that the Mortain casket was intended to hold the Eucharist (*op. cit.* pp. 20 ff.) rather than to serve as a reliquary. Professor Dickins has pointed out to me the interesting parallel between the Mortain form *kiismeel*, with loss of *r*, and the Devonshire place-name Kismeldon.

[2] The names in parentheses are the Old English equivalents as found in the poem *Deor*, ed. by Kemp Malone (London, 1933). For the story itself see the eddic *Vǫlundarkviþa* and *Þiðriks Saga*, chs. 57 ff.

[3] For a different interpretation of the Vǫlundr panel, cf., for example, P. W. Souers, 'The Wayland Scene on the Franks Casket', *Speculum*, vol. 18 (1943), pp. 104 ff.

The right panel presents the Christian subject of the Adoration of the Magi, the runes ᛗᚪᚷᛁ *mægi* appearing in the top centre of the panel.

A consecutive runic inscription in alliterative verse runs around three sides of the two panels but bears no relation to the figure subjects. It begins in the upper left-hand corner, continues along the top, down the right-hand side, and then along the bottom where the runes read and face from right to left. Reading upwards along the left-hand side are nine more runes which are linked in sense to the rest but do not form part of the two preceding alliterative verses. The runes are as follows:

Top: ᚠᛁᛋᚳ · ᚠᛚᚩᛞᚢ · ᚪᚻᚩᚠᚩᚾᚠᛖᚱᚷ

  f i s c . f l o d u . a h o f o n f e r g

Right side: ᛖᚾᛒᛖᚱᛁᚷ

  e n b e r i g

Bottom (for convenience I have reversed the runes to read and face from left to right):

ᚹᚪᚱᚦᚷᚪ: ᛋᚱᛁᚳᚷᚱᚩᚱᚾᚦᚪᚱᚻᛖᚩᚾᚷᚱᛖᚢᛏᚷᛁᛋᚹᚩᛗ

w a r þ g a : s r i c g r o r n þ æ r h e o n g r e u t g i s w o m

Left side: ᚻᚱᚩᚾᚫᛋᛒᚪᚾ

  h r o n æ s b a n

Divided into words and transcribed into lines of verse the inscription reads:

> Fisc flodu ahof on fergenberig;
> warþ gasric grorn, þær he on greut giswom.
> Hronæs ban.

> The flood lifted up the fish on to the cliff-bank;
> the whale became sad, where he swam on the shingle.
> Whale's bone.

This clearly bears no relation to the figure subjects and may properly be regarded as referring to the whale cast upon the (?Northumbrian) shore and to the casket made of its bone. The reading of the runes themselves presents no difficulty, but commentators have differed widely on questions of interpretation.[1] The main points are these: some have regarded *hronæs ban*

---

[1] For details, see Dobbie, *The Anglo-Saxon Minor Poems*, pp. 204f.

7-2

as the beginning of the inscription and thus as part of the first line of verse, taking *fisc flodu* as a compound noun and rendering 'the fish-flood lifted the whale's bones on to the mainland'. The view here favoured appears preferable, however, both on metrical grounds and because the other alliterative verse inscription on the right side of the casket also begins in the top left corner. The word *gasric* has been variously interpreted as 'ocean', 'rager, impetuous creature', 'spear-wounded', or 'whale', and *grorn* as either 'turbid' or 'sad'. One cannot be dogmatic in such matters, but it will be admitted that the interpretation here favoured yields perfectly acceptable sense.

Linguistically interesting forms are *flōdu*, 'flood', still retaining final *-u* after a long stem syllable,[1] and *greut*, 'grit, sand, shingle', with *eu* for normal Old English *ēo*.[2] The runes present no difficulties, but we might note these points: ᛗ *d* is the more archaic of the forms current in Anglo-Saxon usage; the main stroke of *n* is carved at a slant in every case; ᚷ *g* is used indiscriminately for front and back sounds in contrast, for example, to the treatment on the Ruthwell Cross.

Back (Fig. 44).

The back of the casket depicts the following subjects:

(1) A central scene shows a large shrine-like structure which occupies nearly the whole height of the panel. Bruce Dickins has suggested that this represents 'the Temple, containing the Ark of the Covenant with poles for carrying it: on either side the Cherubim and, underneath, the oxen below the sea of brass (I Kings vii. 44)'.[3]

(2) Top left: this depicts the capture of Jerusalem in the year 70, showing Titus, with a group of spearmen behind him, striking with his sword at one of the defenders.

(3) Top right: here a group of people, including some women, is shown fleeing from the city.

(4) Bottom left: a trial scene is depicted with a central figure, probably that of the judge, seated on a throne. Immedi-

---

[1] Sievers–Brunner, *op. cit.* para. 146 and note.

[2] *Ibid.* para. 77.

[3] *British Museum Guide to Anglo-Saxon Antiquities* (1923), p. 97.

ately to the left, at the bottom left corner of the panel, occur the
runes ᛗᛟᛗ *dom*, 'doom, judgement', which presumably refer
to the adjoining scene.

(5) Bottom right: this shows a group of eight figures, probably representing important captives. The runes ᚷᛁᛋᛚ *gisl*,
'hostage' in the bottom right corner of the panel presumably
refer to this group.

Apart from the two runic words in the two lower corners
just mentioned, two inscriptions, partly in runes, partly in
Roman letters, run along the top and the two sides of the panel.
The first begins on the left side, reading upwards, and continues across the top of the Titus-scene to which it refers.

Left side: ᚻᛖᚱᚠᛖᚷᛏᚪᚦ

                h e r f e g t a þ

Top: ᛏᛁᛏᚢᛋᛖᚾᚷᛁᚢᚦᛖᚪᛋᚢ

          t i t u s e n d g i u þ e a s u

which means, divided into words: 'her fegtaþ titus end
giuþeasu', 'here fight Titus and the Jews'.

The second inscription refers to the flight of the inhabitants,
the figure subject on the top right; it consists of Roman letters
running along the top of this scene and of runes reading downwards on the right-hand side.

Top: HIC FUGIANT HIERUSALIM

Right side: ᚠᚪᛁᛏᚪᛏᚪᚱᛖᛋ

                a f i t a t o r e s

that is: 'hic fugiant [*for* fugiunt] Hierusalim afitatores [*for* habi-
tatores]', 'here the inhabitants flee from Jerusalem'.

It is difficult to explain why on this side of the casket alone
Roman letters are employed, unless we assume that the carver
had in mind or was working from a Latin text and inadvertently
slipped into using Roman letters at this point, corrected himself
when continuing down the right-hand side, but logically
enough completed his sentence in Latin. We have already noted
that on the Ruthwell Cross one of the isolated words is Latin
though written in runes (above p. 94). The spelling *afitatores*

shows the not uncommon dropping of the initial aspirate and the use of *f* to indicate probably the sound [v].

Linguistic points to note are: (i) the spelling *gt* for [çt] in *fegtaþ* represents a variant besides *ct* (cf. Lancaster), *cht*, and the normal Old English *ht*[1] (cf. also the use of -ᛁᛏᛏ- in *almeᵹttig* on Ruthwell); (ii) the form *end* for *and* or *ond* occurs in some early manuscripts[2] and presumably represents a quite normal alternative form; and (iii) *giuþeasu*: this is a most abnormal form for the nominative plural 'Jews'; *giuþeas* might have been expected, perhaps even intended, the *u* having been added in error, or as Souers puts it 'merely arbitrarily appended'.[3] Bradley suggested that the carver possibly meant to write *giuþea sumæ*, 'some of the Jews', but had no more room for the two final runes.

The runes themselves on this side present no unusual features; the use of ᚷ *g* in *fegtaþ* has just been commented upon; its use in *giuþeasu* should be compared with that in *gessus*, 'Jesus', on the west face of the Bewcastle Cross.

Left side (Fig. 45).

This side of the casket is damaged, but the figure panel is intact and the runic inscription running right round it can be read without great difficulty. The panel illustrates a classical subject: in the centre the suckling of Romulus and Remus by the she-wolf, with another wolf above 'for the sake of a balance in the design',[4] and on each side two figures of men armed with spears, identified by Souers as Faustulus with three other shepherds discovering the twins.

The inscription probably starts, as on the front and right sides of the casket, in the upper left corner, continuing along the top, down the right side, along the bottom and up the left-hand side. The runes along the bottom are upside down. This line ends with a set of dots which some commentators take as signifying the end of the whole inscription, but which probably served simply to fill up the empty space at the end of the line.

[1] Sievers–Brunner, *op. cit.* para. 221.1 and n. 1.
[2] *Ibid.* para. 79, n. 4.
[3] In *Harvard Studies and Notes in Philology and Literature*, vol. 17 (1935), p. 166.
[4] *Ibid.* vol. 18 (1935), p. 207.

As this inscription is not in alliterative verse one cannot be dogmatic as to whether the words *oþlæ unneg* on the left are the beginning or the end of the inscription; the sense, in either case, remains unaffected. The inscription reads:

Top: ᚱ ᚪ ᛗ ᚹ ᚪ ᛚ ᚢ ᛋ ᚪ ᚾ ᛞ ᚱ ᛖ ᚢ ᛗ ᚹ ᚪ ᛚ ᚢ ᛋ ᛏ ᚹ

      r o m w a l u s a n d r e u m w a l u s t w

      ᚩ ᚷ ᛖ ᚾ

      œ g e n

Right side: ᚷ ᛁ ᛒ ᚱ ᚩ ᚦ ᚪ ᚱ

      g i b r o þ æ r .

Bottom: ᚠ ᚪ ᚩ ᛞ ᛞ ᚫ ᚻ ᛁ ᚫ ᚹ ᚣ ᛚ ᛁ ᚠ ᛁ ᚾ ᚱ ᚩ ᛗ ᚫ ᚳ ᚫ ᛋ

      a fœ d d æ h i æ w y l i f i n r o m æ c æs

      ᛏ ᚱ ᛁ :

      t r i :

Left side: ᚩ ᚦ ᛚ ᚢ ᚾ ᚷ ᚷ ᛖ ᚷ

      o þ l æ u n n e g

that is: 'romwalus and reumwalus twœgen gibroþær: afœddæ hiæ wylif in romæ cæstri, oþlæ unneg', 'Romulus and Remus, two brothers: a she-wolf fed them in Rome city, far from their native land'.

Linguistic points worth noting are: the characteristically Anglian use of *æ*;[1] the monophthong in *cæstri* (West-Saxon *ceaster*)[2] and its dative ending *-i* (cf. above, p. 80); the intrusive vowel in *wylif* (cf. *-berig* on the front of the casket and above, pp. 86 f.); and the form *gibroþær*, a perfectly good Northumbrian equivalent of Old Saxon *gibroðer*.

The runes are again quite straightforward; as in *fegtaþ* ᚷ *g* is used for the spirant in *unneg*; the double consonants in *unneg* and *afœddæ* are written as such according to usual manuscript rather than traditional runic practice.

Right side (Fig. 46).

The right side whose original is in Florence consists of one continuous figure-panel, with three runic words inscribed within it, and a runic inscription surrounding it. The figure-

---

[1] Sievers–Brunner, *op. cit.* para. 101.
[2] *Ibid.* para. 91*a*.

carving is quite plain, but its significance has been much discussed and hotly debated. By far the most attractive explanation (first suggested by Söderberg in 1890 and elaborated by Wadstein in 1900) relates it to the Northern Sigurðr (Sigurd, Siegfried) story.[1] This we can, I think, accept in principle. In detail, however, no fully satisfactory solution has been advanced, particularly for the episode represented on the left of the panel.

Here we have a human figure with an animal's head, sitting on a little mound and facing an armed warrior. This mysterious figure which has puzzled so many beholders seems to me quite a creditable attempt at representing pictorially a man turned animal; this, in the Sigurðr story, can only be Fáfnir, brother of Reginn, who became a dragon and appropriated and guarded the treasure of Andvari. It is on his treasure hoard, I suggest, that he is here shown sitting. The armed figure facing him can then only be Sigurðr himself, the slayer of Fáfnir, not, as some have suggested, Hǫgni who was one of the three brothers responsible for Sigurðr's death. Sigurðr might have been expected to carry his sword Gramr with which he slew the dragon, but we learn from one tradition that he also carried a spear, for he used it to roast the slain Fáfnir's heart.[2]

The centre portion of the panel shows a horse, his head bent, looking down upon a mound with a human body inside it. To the right appears a human figure, evidently a woman. This scene is generally taken to represent Sigurðr's wife Guðrún (Gudrun) and his horse Grani mourning over the slain hero's grave. It is thus that both are described in the eddic Guðrúnarkviþa II, 4 f., 11 f.[3] The runic inscription on this side of the casket seems to bear this out.

Finally, on the right of the panel, stand three heavily-cloaked human figures, whom Wadstein took to be Brynhildr, who instigated Sigurðr's murder, and the brothers Gunnarr and Hǫgni, who helped to bring it about. All three figures may,

---

[1] Well-known, though later, examples of episodes from the Sigurðr story are the carvings on the non-runic crosses at Leeds Parish Church and Halton (Lancs) of the late tenth or early eleventh century.

[2] Cf. the prose passage after st. 31 in the eddic Fáfnismál.

[3] Cf. also the eddic Brot af Sigurðarkviþo, 7.

however, be women, and other possibilities occur to one: such as that the figures represent the Nornir, the 'three fatal sisters' of Northern mythology. Or else one might relate this picture very tentatively to a tradition only represented in the admittedly much later eddic *Guðrúnarkviþa I*. Here it is related that three noble ladies, Giaflaug, Herborg, and Gullrǫnd, came to share Guðrún's grief and comfort her in her distress. Of course this Icelandic poem is centuries later than the Franks casket,[1] yet it may represent a particular tradition not recorded elsewhere; the Egill episode on the lid of the casket is not preserved in any literary record. We also know that variant traditions exist, for example, of the place and circumstances of Sigurðr's death; so that it is not wholly unlikely that the medieval Icelandic poem preserves an older tradition for which this English carving is our only other evidence.

The main runic inscription is as difficult and disputed as the figure carving. Beginning in the upper left-hand corner it runs along the top, down the right side, along the bottom where the runes are upside down, and finishes going upwards on the left-hand side. A unique feature of the inscription on this side of the casket is its use of the following arbitrary vowel-runes:

ᚻ *a*, ᚪ *æ*, ᚷ *e*, ᛁ *i*, ᚻ *o*.

Normal vowel-runes occur only twice in the main inscription: ᛖ *e* in *særden*, and ᚱ *a* in the ligature ᚠ̆ *fa* in *sefa*, where Napier preferred to read *sefu*. In the three short words carved in runes within the figure-panel itself, however, the normal vowel-runes only are employed. These words will be considered later. The main inscription reads:

Top: ᚻ ᚷ ᚱ·ᚻ ᚻ ᛚ·ᛚ ᛁ ᛏ ᚪ ᚦ·ᚻ ᚷ ᚻ ᚪ ᚱ ᛗ ᛒ ᚷ ᚱ ᚷ ᚪ·ᚻ

h e r h o s s i t æ þ o n h æ r m b e r g æ a

ᚷ ᛁ

g l . .

Right side: ᛞ ᚱ ᛁ ᚷ ᛁ ᚦ·ᚻ ᚹ ᚪ·

d r i g i þ s w æ

---

[1] G. Turville-Petre, *Origins of Icelandic Literature* (Oxford, 1953), p. 14: eleventh or twelfth century.

Bottom: ᚺᛂᚱᛉ ᚷᚱᛏᚺᚷ ᚷᛂᚻᚷᚱᚼᚠᚻᛁᚱᛗᛖᚾᚻ

hiri,erta,e,gi sgraf,sær,d ens

ᚻᚱᚷᛁᚺ

o rgæ,a

Left side: ᚷᛗᚻᚷᚴᛏᚻᚱᚷᛁ

n d,s e fâ,t o r næ

This may be transcribed into three lines of alliterative verse:

> her hos sitæþ on hærmbergæ
> agl.. drigiþ; swæ hiri erta egi sgraf,
> særden sorgæ and sefa tornæ.

The interpretation of these lines, however, is beset with difficulties,[1] and a fresh study of them must be reserved for another occasion. The most plausible rendering hitherto advanced is:

> Here the horse stands above the mound of woe,
> It suffers tribulation; just as to her Erta appointed anxiety,
> A grave of grief, in sorrow and anguish of heart.

But this is not by any means satisfactory, for these reasons: *hors*, 'horse', for *hos* is at best a doubtful emendation; *sitæþ* should read *sitiþ* (like *drigiþ*), but if it refers to the standing horse of the carving it cannot mean 'sits'; *hiri* could be a variant of Anglian *hiræ*, 'to her', in which case Guðrún is most likely meant. *Erta* is quite uncertain: it has been connected with *Erce*, the 'earth-mother' whose name survives in one of the Anglo-Saxon metrical charms,

Erce, Erce, Erce, eorþan modor,[2]

and could perhaps be connected with Sigurðr's earthen grave, but all this is very tenuous; *egi sgraf* makes sense if we assume that *egi* is an earlier form of O.E. *ege*, 'fear, anxiety', and that it is the object of *sgraf*, the past tense of *scrīfan*, 'to appoint, prescribe', the carver using *g* for *c* because the normal *c*-rune here figures with the value *a*; *særden*, 'grave of grief', is not very satisfactory either; Napier, followed by Bruce Dickins, suggested that ᛗ here represents *æ*, reading *sær dæn*, 'rendered miserable'.

---

[1] For details, cf. Dobbie, *op. cit.* pp. 205 ff.
[1] 'For Unfruitful Land', 51 (*ibid.* p. 117).

It is indeed a miserable harvest of doubts and uncertainties, but such a meagre result need not discourage one unduly: surely the puzzle of these runes will one day be solved.

The use on this side of the casket of arbitrary runes to designate vowels can only be explained as a personal whim or a touch of mystery. Cryptic or 'secret' runes occasionally occur, as we have seen, in Scandinavian and English inscriptions, such as the Hackness *hahal*-runes or the various secret runes on the Swedish Rök stone. On the casket their use is not wholly consistent, for several normal vowel-runes occur, and the three words inscribed within the figure panel employ the ordinary Anglo-Saxon vowel-runes. The first of these words, ᚹᚢᛞᚢ *wudu*, 'wood', is below the figure of the horse, and is presumably a reference to the scene depicted: according to one tradition (*Guðrúnarkviþa II*, 11 f.) Sigurðr was slain in a wood.

The second word is carved above the horse's back and reads ᚱᛁᛋᚳᛁ *risci*, most likely the Old English word *risce*, 'rush, reed, twig', perhaps another reference to the scene of Sigurðr's slaying. Or else it could refer to the Fáfnir episode; for it was on the way to the water where Fáfnir was wont to creep, and where presumably rushes grew, that Sigurðr dug the pit which trapped the dragon. Such a pit would have had to be covered with rushes to conceal it from the intended victim.[1] In the picture the man-dragon actually holds what may be twigs or rushes in his hands, but the significance of this (if any) I cannot determine.

The last of the three words is inscribed above the heads of the horse and the sorrowing woman; it reads ᛒᛁᛏᚪ *bita*, an Old English word meaning 'that which bites, an animal'.[2] Most likely this refers to the horse pictured just below.

One cannot help realising just how many doubts remain concerning the interpretation of both pictures and runes on this side of the Franks casket. On the whole, however, the connec-

---

[1] According to *Fáfnismál* Sigurðr himself waited inside the pit; according to *Vǫlsunga Saga*, ch. 18, Sigurðr dug several pits.

[2] F. Holthausen, *Altengl. Etymol. Wörterbuch* (Halle, 1934), s.v., glosses 'Beisser, wildes Tier'. Bosworth–Toller, *Anglo-Saxon Dictionary*, s.v., gloss *ferus* and quote a couple of O.E. compounds denoting insects.

tion with episodes in the Sigurðr story offers an attractive and plausible solution, and we may conclude that the pictures illustrate three separate scenes, that the three words in the panel most probably all belong to the central one, and that the surrounding inscription is a brief verse commentary on the picture panel. The story of Sigurðr was common Germanic property and just as in the Sigmund passage in *Beowulf* (857 ff.), so in the present instance a few seemingly disconnected allusions probably sufficed to recall the salient outlines of a familiar story.

The date and provenance of the Franks casket have been established beyond reasonable doubt by Napier's linguistic analysis. The language is unmistakably Anglian and certain forms limit it further to Northumbria, and, in point of time, to the early eighth century. On runological grounds this date and provenance are equally acceptable; we have seen that (the nonce runes apart, of course) all the runes belong to the common Anglo-Saxon twenty-eight-letter fuþorc. Runes of the later Northumbrian extension do not occur.

The runes, like the figure carving, are primarily ornamental. It was probably quite natural for an early eighth-century Northumbrian artist to associate runic writing with figure motifs drawn from Germanic legend; what is surprising is that he made so little use of Roman letters, especially in connection with the scenes derived from classical and biblical sources. Our conclusion must be that Englishmen of that time continued to cherish the traditions of their forefathers and were fully aware not only of the ancient dignity of the fuþorc but of something of its age-old mystery. We can indeed be thankful that to this day the Franks casket survives as a unique and priceless specimen of our own runic heritage.

Bibliography

WADSTEIN, E. *The Clermont Runic Casket*. Skrifter utgifna av K. Humanistiska Vetenskaps-Samfundet i Uppsala, vol. 6, pt. 7. Uppsala, 1900.

VIËTOR, W. *Das angelsächsische Runenkästchen aus Auzon—The Anglo-Saxon Runic Casket*. German and English text. Marburg, 1901.

NAPIER, A. S. 'The Franks Casket.' *An English Miscellany presented to Dr Furnivall*, pp. 362 ff. Oxford, 1901.

BROWN, G. B. *The Arts in Early England*, vol. 6, pt. 1, ch. 2. London, 1930.

SOUERS, P. W. 'The Top of the Franks Casket.' *Harvard Studies and Notes in Philology and Literature*, vol. 17, pp. 163 ff. 1935.

—— 'The Franks Casket: Left Side.' *Ibid*. vol. 18, pp. 199 ff. 1935.

—— 'The Magi on the Franks Casket.' *Ibid*. vol. 19, pp. 249 ff. 1937.

—— 'The Wayland Scene on the Franks Casket.' *Speculum*, vol. 18, pp. 104 ff. 1943.

SELECT BIBLIOGRAPHY

I. BIBLIOGRAPHICAL

HERMANNSSON, H. *Catalogue of Runic Literature, forming a part of the Icelandic Collection bequeathed by Willard Fiske* (Cornell Univ. Library). Oxford, 1918.

ARNTZ, H. *Bibliographie der Runenkunde.* Leipzig, 1937.

BONSER, W. *An Anglo-Saxon and Celtic Bibliography (450–1087).* Oxford, 1957,

MARQUARDT, H. *Bibliographie der Runeninschriften nach Fundorten,* vol. 1: Die Runeninschriften der Britischen Inseln. (In preparation.)

II. COLLECTIONS OF RUNIC INSCRIPTIONS

STEPHENS, G. *The Old-Northern Runic Monuments of Scandinavia and England,* 4 vols. London and Copenhagen, 1866–1901.

—— *Handbook of the Old-Northern Runic Monuments of Scandinavia and England.* London and Copenhagen, 1884.

HENNING, R. *Die deutschen Runendenkmäler.* Strassburg, 1889.

BUGGE, S. AND OLSEN, M. *Norges Indskrifter med de ældre Runer,* 4 vols. Christiania, 1891–1924.

WIMMER, L. F. A. *De danske Runemindesmærker,* 4 vols. Copenhagen, 1893–1908.

—— 'De tyske Runemindesmærker.' *Aarbøger for nordisk Oldkyndighed og Historie,* pp. 1 ff. 1894.

VIËTOR, W. *Die northumbrischen Runensteine.* Marburg, 1895.

SÖDERBERG, S., BRATE, E., WESSÉN, E. AND OTHERS. *Sveriges Runinskrifter (utgivna av Kungl. Vitterhets Historie och Antikvitets Akademien).* Stockholm, 1900–.

KERMODE, P. M. C. *Manx Crosses.* London, 1907.

DICKINS, B. *Runic and Heroic Poems of the Old Teutonic Peoples.* Cambridge, 1915.

MARSTRANDER, C. J. S. 'De gotiske runeminnesmerker.' *Norsk tidsskrift for sprogvidenskap,* vol. 3, pp. 25 ff. 1929.

KRAUSE, W. *Runeninschriften im Älteren Futhark.* Halle, 1937.

ARNTZ, H. AND ZEISS, H. *Die einheimischen Runendenkmäler des Festlandes.* Gesamtausgabe der älteren Runendenkmäler, vol. 1. Leipzig, 1939.

OLSEN, M. AND OTHERS. *Norges innskrifter med de yngre runer.* Oslo, 1941–.

BÆKSTED, A. *Islands Runeindskrifter.* Bibl. Arnamagnæana, vol. 2. Copenhagen, 1942.

JACOBSEN, L. AND MOLTKE, E. *Danmarks Runeindskrifter*, 3 vols. Copenhagen, 1941–2.

MARSTRANDER, C. J. S. 'De nordiske runeinnskrifter i eldre alfabet.' *Viking*, vol. 16, pp. 1 ff. 1953.

OLSEN, M. 'Runic Inscriptions in Great Britain, Ireland and the Isle of Man.' *Viking Antiquities in Great Britain and Ireland*, vol. 6, pp. 151 ff. Oslo, 1954.

III. GENERAL WORKS

GRIMM, W. K. *Über deutsche Runen*. Göttingen, 1821.

WIMMER, L. F. A. 'Runeskriftens Oprindelse og Udvikling i Norden.' *Aarbøger for nordisk Oldkyndighed og Historie*, pp. 1 ff. 1874.

TAYLOR, I. *Greeks and Goths: A Study on the Runes*. London, 1879.

WIMMER, L. F. A. *Die Runenschrift*. Translated from the Danish by F. Holthausen. Berlin, 1887.

SIEVERS, E. 'Runen und Runeninschriften.' Paul's *Grundriss der germ. Philologie²*, vol. 1, pp. 248 ff. Strassburg, 1901.

PAUES, A. C. 'Runes and Manuscripts.' *The Cambridge History of English Literature*, vol. 1, pp. 7 ff. 1907.

JÓNSSON, F. 'Runerne i den norsk-islandske Digtning og Litteratur.' *Aarbøger for nordisk Oldkyndighed og Historie*, pp. 283 ff. 1910.

BROWN, G. B. *The Arts in Early England*, vols. 3–6. London, 1915–37.

JÓHANNESSON, A. *Grammatik der urnordischen Runeninschriften*. Heidelberg, 1923.

GORDON, E. V. *An Introduction to Old Norse*. Oxford, 1927 (2nd ed. revised by A. R. Taylor, 1957).

FRIESEN, O. v. 'Runes.' *Encycl. Brit.* (14th ed.), vol. 19. 1929.

FRIESEN, O. v. AND OTHERS. *Runorna*. Nordisk Kultur, vol. 6. Stockholm, etc. 1933.

DIECKHOFF, A. D. *Einführung in die nordische Runenlehre*. Hamburg, 1935.

ARNTZ, H. *Handbuch der Runenkunde*. Halle, 1935 (2nd ed. 1944).

SHETELIG, H. AND FALK, H. *Scandinavian Archaeology*, trans. E. V. Gordon. Oxford, 1937.

ARNTZ, H. *Die Runenschrift, ihre Geschichte und ihre Denkmäler*. Halle, 1938.

Beiträge zur Runenkunde und nordischen Sprachwissenschaft. Festschrift für G. Neckel. Leipzig, 1938.

WEBER, E. *Kleine Runenkunde*. Berlin, 1941.

BLOMFIELD, J. 'Runes and the Gothic Alphabet.' *Saga-Book of the Viking Soc. for Northern Research*, vol. 12, pp. 177 ff., 209 ff. 1941–2.

KRAUSE, W. *Was man in Runen ritzte*, 2nd ed. Halle, 1943.

BÆKSTED, A. *Runerne. Deres Historie og Brug.* Copenhagen, 1943.

IV. ORIGIN OF RUNES

WIMMER, L. F. A. 'Runeskriftens Oprindelse og Udvikling i Norden.' *Aarbøger for nordisk Oldkyndighed og Historie.* 1874.

FRIESEN, O. V. 'Om runskriftens härkomst.' *Språkvet. Sällsk. i Uppsala förhandl.* Uppsala, 1904.

PEDERSEN, H. 'L'origine des runes.' *Mém. Soc. Roy. Ant. Nord.* pp. 88 ff. 1920–4.

CAHEN, M. 'Origine et développement de l'écriture runique.' *Mém. de la Soc. linguist. de Paris*, vol. 23, pp. 1 ff. 1923.

MARSTRANDER, C. J. S. 'Om runene og runenavnenes oprindelse.' *Norsk tidsskrift for sprogvidenskap*, vol. 1, pp. 85 ff. 1928.

HAMMARSTRÖM, M. 'Om runskriftens härkomst.' *Stud. i nord. filologi*, vol. 20, pp. 1 ff. 1930.

BAESECKE, G. 'Die Herkunft der Runen.' *Germanisch-romanische Monatsschrift*, vol. 22, pp. 413 ff. 1934.

HEMPEL, H. 'Der Ursprung der Runenschrift.' *Ibid.* vol. 23, pp. 401 ff. 1935.

AGRELL, S. *Die Herkunft der Runenschrift.* K. Humanistiska Vetenskapssamfundets i Lund, Årsberättelse 1937–8, 4. Lund, 1938.

ALTHEIM, F. AND TRAUTMANN, E. *Vom Ursprung der Runen.* Frankfurt (Main), 1939.

ALTHEIM, F. AND TRAUTMANN-NEHRIG, E. *Kimbern und Runen.* Berlin, 1943.

ASKEBERG, F. *Norden och kontinenten i gammal tid. Studier i forngermansk kulturhistoria.* Uppsala, 1944.

MOSSÉ, F. 'L'origine de l'écriture runique: état présent de la question.' *Conférences de l'Institut de linguistique de l'Univ. de Paris*, vol. 10, pp. 43 ff. 1951.

V. RUNE-NAMES

GRIENBERGER, T. V. 'Die germanischen Runennamen. I: Die gotischen Buchstabennamen.' *Beiträge zur Gesch. der deutschen Sprache und Literatur*, vol. 21, pp. 185 ff. 1896.

AGRELL, S. *Zur Frage nach dem Ursprung der Runennamen.* Skrifter utg. av Vet.-soc. i Lund, 10. Lund, 1928.

LEYEN, F. V. D. 'Die germanische Runenreihe und ihre Namen.'
Zeitschrift des Vereins für Volkskunde, N.F. 2, pp. 170 ff. 1930.

WRENN, C. L. 'Late Old English Rune-Names.' *Medium Ævum*,
vol. 1, pp. 24 ff. 1932.

JUNGANDREAS, W. 'Die germanische Runenreihe und ihre Bedeutung.' *Zeitschrift f. deutsche Philologie*, vol. 60, pp. 105 ff. 1935.
—— 'Zur Runenreihe.' *Ibid.* vol. 61, pp. 227 ff. 1936.

WRIGHT, C. E. 'A Postscript to "Late Old English Rune-Names".'
Medium Ævum, vol. 5, pp. 149 ff. 1936.

ARNTZ, H. 'Runen und Runennamen.' *Anglia*, vols. 67/68,
pp. 172 ff. 1944.

KRAUSE, W. 'Untersuchungen zu den Runennamen. I. Die
Lauch-Rune. II. Runennamen und Götterwelt.' *Nachr. der
Akad. der Wissenschaften in Göttingen. Philol.-Hist. Klasse*,
pp. 60 ff.; pp. 93 ff. 1946/7, 1948.

SCHNEIDER, K. *Die Germanischen Runennamen. Versuch einer Gesamtdeutung.* Meisenheim am Glan, 1956.

VI. RUNE-MAGIC

GRIMM, J. *Deutsche Mythologie.* Berlin, 1875–8.

HELM, K. *Altgermanische Religionsgeschichte.* Heidelberg, 1913—
53.

OLSEN, M. 'Om troldruner.' *Edda*, vol. 5, pp. 2, 225 ff. 1916.

FEIST, S. 'Runen und Zauberwesen im germanischen Altertum.'
Arkiv f. nordisk filologi, vol. 35, pp. 243 ff. 1919.
—— 'Die religionsgeschichtliche Bedeutung der ältesten Runeninschriften.' *J. Engl. and Germanic Philology*, vol. 21, pp. 602 ff.
1922.

MOGK, E. *Germanische Religionsgeschichte und Mythologie*, 3rd ed.
Berlin, 1927.

BRIX, H. *Studier i nordisk Runemagi. Runemesterkunsten, upplandske
Runestene, Rökstenen, nogle nordiske Runetekster.* Copenhagen,
1928.

PHILIPPSON, E. A. *Germanisches Heidentum bei den Angelsachsen.*
Leipzig, 1929.

BONSER, W. 'Survivals of Paganism in Anglo-Saxon England.'
Trans. Birmingham Archaeol. Soc. vol. 56, pp. 37 ff. 1932.

DICKINS, B. 'English Names and Old English Heathenism.'
Essays and Studies, vol. 19, pp. 148 ff. 1934.

VRIES, J. DE. *Altgermanische Religionsgeschichte.* Berlin–Leipzig,
1935–7 (2nd ed. 1956).

NORDÉN, A. 'Magiska runinskrifter.' *Arkiv f. nordisk filologi*,
vol. 53, pp. 147 ff. 1937.

HEUSLER, A. *Die altgermanische Dichtung*, 2nd ed. Potsdam, 1941.

STORMS, G. *Anglo-Saxon Magic*. The Hague, 1948.

HÖFLER, O. *Germanisches Sakralkönigtum I: Der Runenstein von Rök und die Germanische Individualweihe*. Tübingen and Münster/Köln, 1952.

BÆKSTED, A. *Målruner og troldruner. Runemagiske studier*. Copenhagen, 1952.

GRATTAN, J. H. G. AND SINGER, S. *Anglo-Saxon Magic and Medicine*. London, 1952.

ELLIOTT, R. W. V. 'Runes, Yews, and Magic.' *Speculum*, vol. 32, pp. 250 ff. 1957.

BRANSTON, B. *The Lost Gods of England*. London, 1957.

VII. ENGLISH RUNES AND RUNIC INSCRIPTIONS

(See also the bibliographical references in ch. VII.)

KEMBLE, J. M. 'The Runes of the Anglo-Saxons.' *Archaeologia*, vol. 28, pp. 327 ff. 1840.

SWEET, H. *The Oldest English Texts*. Early English Text Society, o.s. vol. 83, pp. 124 ff. London, 1885.

KEARY, C. F. *A Catalogue of English Coins in the British Museum*. Anglo-Saxon Series, vol. 1, edited by R. S. Poole. London, 1887.

HALL, G. R. 'Notes on a Pre-conquest Memorial Stone from Birtley, and fragments of Crosses from Falstone, North Tynedale.' *Archaeol. Æliana*, vol. 13, pp. 252 ff. 1889.

GRIENBERGER, T. V. 'Die angelsächsischen Runenreihen und die sogenannten Hrabanischen Alphabete.' *Arkiv f. nordisk filologi*, vol. 15, pp. 1 ff. 1899.

CHADWICK, H. M. 'Early Inscriptions in the North of England.' *Trans. Yorkshire Dialect Society*, pt. 3, pp. 79 ff. Bradford, 1901.

GRIENBERGER, T. V. 'Drei Westgermanische Runeninschriften.' *Zeitschrift f. deutsche Philologie*, vol. 41, pp. 419 ff. (Britsum, Derbyshire bone plate, Brunswick casket.) 1909.

British Museum Guide to Anglo-Saxon Antiquities. London, 1923.

PEERS, C. R. 'The Inscribed and Sculptured Stones of Lindisfarne.' *Archaeologia*, vol. 74, pp. 255 ff. 1925.

COLLINGWOOD, W. G. *Northumbrian Crosses of the Pre-Norman Age*. London, 1927.

OLSEN, M. 'Notes on the Urswick Inscription.' *Norsk tidsskrift for sprogvidenskap*, vol. 4, pp. 282 ff. 1930.

HARDER, H. 'Eine angelsächsische Runeninschrift.' *Archiv Stud. neueren Sprachen*, vol. 160, pp. 87 ff. (Runic rings in the British Museum.) 1931.

DICKINS, B. 'A System of Transliteration for Old English Runic Inscriptions.' *Leeds Studies in English*, vol. 1, pp. 15 ff. 1932.

—— 'The *epa* Coins.' *Ibid.* pp. 20 f. 1932.

SISAM, K. 'Cynewulf and his poetry.' *Proc. Brit. Acad.* vol. 18, pp. 303 ff. 1932. (Reprinted in Sisam, *Studies in the History of Old English Literature*, Oxford, 1953.)

ROSS, A. S. C. 'O.E. gebidæþ.' *Mod. Lang. Notes*, vol. 47, p. 377. (Lancaster, Urswick, Falstone.) 1932.

HARDER, H. 'Die Runen der angelsächsischen Schwertinschrift im Brit. Museum.' *Archiv Stud. neueren Sprachen*, vol. 161, pp. 86 f. (Chessel Down.) 1932.

—— 'Die Runeninschrift der Silberspange von Sheffield.' *Archiv Stud. neueren Sprachen*, vol. 164, pp. 250 ff. 1933.

DICKINS, B. 'Runic Rings and Old English Charms.' *Archiv Stud. neueren Sprachen*, vol. 167, p. 252. 1935.

ROSS, A. S. C. 'Notes on the Runic Stones at Holy Island.' *Engl. Studien*, vol. 70, pp. 36 ff. 1935–6.

HARDER, H. 'Inschriften angelsächsischer Runenringe.' *Archiv Stud. neueren Sprachen*, vol. 169, pp. 224 ff. 1936.

KELLER, W. 'Zur Chronologie der altenglischen Runen.' *Anglia*, vol. 62, pp. 24 ff. 1938.

DICKINS, B. AND ROSS, A. S. C. 'The Alnmouth Cross.' *Journ. Engl. and Germanic Philology*, vol. 39, pp. 169 ff. 1940.

BENNETT, J. A. W. 'The Beginnings of Runic Studies in England.' *Saga-Book of the Viking Soc. for Northern Research*, vol. 13, pt. IV, pp. 269 ff. 1950–1.

ELLIOTT, R. W. V. 'Cynewulf's Runes in *Christ II* and *Elene*.' *English Studies*, vol. 34, pp. 49 ff. 1953.

—— 'Cynewulf's Runes in *Juliana* and *Fates of the Apostles*.' *Ibid.* pp. 193 ff. 1953.

DEROLEZ, R. *Runica Manuscripta. The English Tradition.* Brugge, 1954.

ELLIOTT, R. W. V. 'The Runes in *The Husband's Message*.' *J. Engl. and Germanic Philol.* vol. 54, pp. 1 ff. 1955.

BRUCE-MITFORD, R. L. S. 'Late Saxon Disc-Brooches.' *Dark-Age Britain* (Studies presented to E. T. Leeds). (Pp. 193 ff. the Sutton Brooch.) London, 1956.

ELLIOTT, R. W. V. 'Two neglected English runic inscriptions: Gilton and Overchurch.' *Mélanges de Linguistique et de Philologie* (Fernand Mossé In Memoriam). Paris, 1959.

Map 1. English Runic Monuments

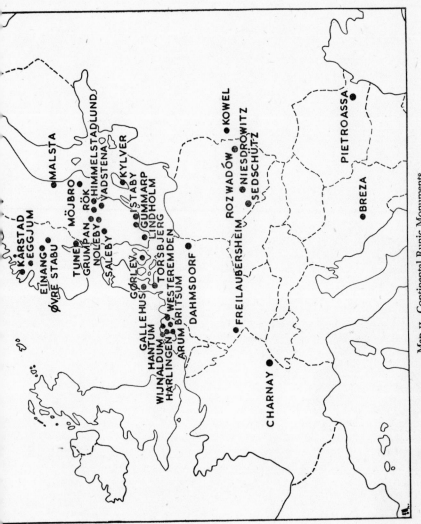

Map II. Continental Runic Monuments

INDEX OF INSCRIPTIONS

GENERAL INDEX

PLATE I

Fig. 1. The Negau helmet. 3rd century B.C. North Italic letters

Fig. 2. The Negau helmet, detail

PLATE II

Fig. 3. The Kylver stone. Gothic; 5th century

Fig. 4. The Vadstena bracteate.
Swedish; 6th century

Fig. 5. The Grumpan bracteate.
Swedish; 6th century

PLATE III

Fig. 6.   The Charnay fibula.
Frankish; 6th century

Fig. 7 *left and right*.   The Thames scramasax.
English; 9th century

PLATE IV

Fig. 8.   The Øvre Stabu spearhead.
(?) Marcommanic; 3rd century

Fig. 9.   The Arum wooden sword.   Frisian; 6th to 7th century

Fig. 10 *left and right*.   The Chessel Down sword hilt.   English; ca. 700

PLATE V

Fig. 11.   The Scanomodu coin.
English; 6th century

Fig. 12.   The Harlingen
(Hada) coin. Frisian;
6th century

Fig. 13.   Pada coin. English
(Mercian); ca. 655

Fig. 14.   Æthelred coin.
English (Mercian); ca. 700

Fig. 15.   Beonna Rex coin. English
(East Anglian); ca. 760

Fig. 16.   Æthelberht: Lul coin.
English (East Anglian); ca. 790

PLATE VI

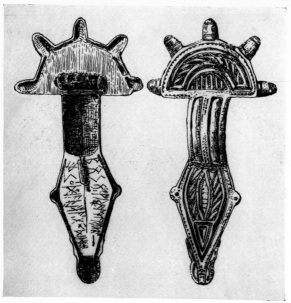

Fig. 17.   The Freilaubersheim fibula. Frankish; 6th century

Fig. 18.   Amulet ring. English;
9th century

Fig. 19.   The Lindholm amulet.
Swedish; 6th century

PLATE VII

Fig. 20.   The Wijnaldum amulet.
Frisian; 6th century

Fig. 21.   The Britsum yew staff. Frisian; 6th to 7th century

PLATE VIII

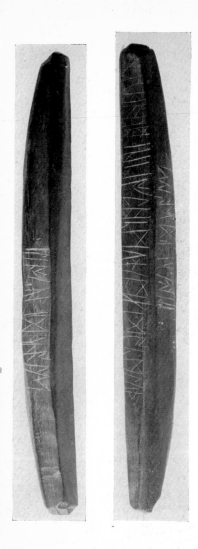

Fig. 22 *left*. The Westeremden yew wand.
Frisian; ca. 800

Fig. 23 *right and below*.
The Westeremden weaving slay.
Frisian; ca. 800

PLATE IX

Fig. 24. The Hantum bone piece. Frisian; early 8th century

Fig. 25. The Derbyshire bone piece. English; 8th century

PLATE X

Fig. 26. The Sandwich stone.
English; 7th century

Fig. 27. The Sandwich stone, detail

PLATE XI

Fig. 28. The Noleby stone. Swedish; 6th century

Fig. 29. The Istaby stone. Swedish; 7th century

PLATE XII

Fig. 30. The Hartlepool pillow-stone.
English; 8th century

Fig. 31. The Dover stone. English; ca. 900

PLATE XIII

Fig. 32   The Falstone stone.   English; 8th century

PLATE XIV

Fig. 34. The Lancaster cross fragment. English; 8th century

Fig. 33. The Hackness cross fragment. English; 8th century

PLATE XV

Fig. 35. The Thornhill cross fragment A.
English; ca. 800. (Runes traced)

Fig. 36. The Thornhill cross
fragment B. English; ca. 800.
(Runes traced)

Fig. 37. The Thornhill cross
fragment C. English; ca. 800

PLATE XVI

Fig. 38. The Ruthwell Cross: West
and South faces. English;
early 8th century

PLATE XVII

Fig. 39. The Ruthwell Cross:
West face, detail

Fig. 40. The Ruthwell Cross:
East face, detail

PLATE XVIII

Fig. 41.   The Bewcastle Cross: main runic panel.
English; early 8th century

PLATE XIX

Fig. 42. The Franks Casket. English; 8th century. Lid

PLATE XX

Fig. 43: The Franks Casket: Front

PLATE XXI

Fig. 44. The Franks Casket: Back

PLATE XXII

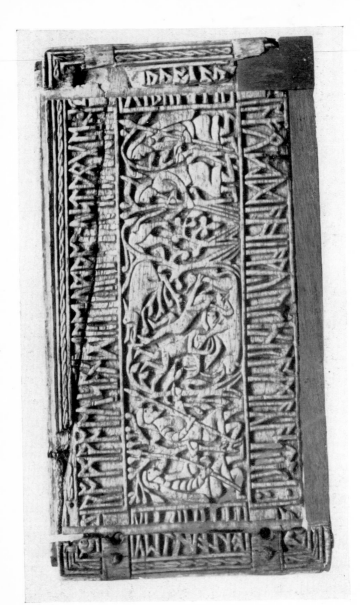

Fig. 45. The Franks Casket: Left side

PLATE XXIII

Fig. 46. The Franks Casket: Right side

PLATE XXIV

Fig. 47. The Lincoln comb case. English; 11th century; Scandinavian runes